EYEWITNESS TRAVEL

TOP 10
LAS VEGAS

CONNIE EMERSON

Top 10 Las Vegas Highlights

The Top 10 of Everything

DK | Penguin Random House

CONTENTS

Las Vegas Area by Area

Streetsmart

Within each Top 10 list in this book, no hierarchy of quality or popularity is implied. All 10 are, in the editor's opinion, of roughly equal merit.

Throughout this book, floors are referred to in accordance with American usage; i.e., the "first floor" is at ground level.

Front cover and spine Neon signs on Fremont Street at dusk
Back cover The glittering skyline of Las Vegas at night
Title page Hotels and casinos lining the famous Strip

The information in this DK Eyewitness Top 10 Travel Guide is checked regularly. Every effort has been made to ensure that this book is as up-to-date as possible at the time of going to press. Some details, however, such as telephone numbers, opening hours, prices, gallery hanging arrangements, and travel information are liable to change. The publishers cannot accept responsibility for any consequences arising from the use of this book, nor for any material on third party websites, and cannot guarantee that any website address in this book will be a suitable source of travel information. We value the views and suggestions of our readers very highly. Please write to: Publisher, DK Eyewitness Travel Guides, Dorling Kindersley, 80 Strand, London WC2R 0RL, Great Britain, or email travelguides@dk.com

Welcome to
Las Vegas

Las Vegas is the most full-on, 24-hour city you could ever hope to visit. It was built as a playground of extravagant casino resorts, top shows, and fine restaurants – a place to have fun and simply forget the world beyond. With Eyewitness Top 10 Las Vegas, it's all yours to enjoy.

More than 40 million tourists pour into Las Vegas each year. The vast majority spend their time on either **the Strip** – the legendary 4-mile (6-km) stretch of Las Vegas Boulevard that is home to the largest casino resorts – or in **Downtown Las Vegas**, the original city core that has its own cluster of smaller, but arguably more characterful, casinos. However, there are also the surrounding deserts to explore, whether you just take an early-morning hike in **Red Rock Canyon** or head further afield to **Zion National Park** or the **Grand Canyon**.

It is perfectly possible to visit Las Vegas and not gamble, but there is no avoiding the **casinos**. They are at the root of everything, holding almost all the city's hotel rooms, plus its best restaurants, bars, nightclubs, theaters, and concert arenas. Above all that, the casinos simply *are* the sights of Las Vegas. They are the weird and wonderful structures that everyone comes to see – the giant pyramid of **Luxor**, the miniature cities of **New York-New York** and **The Venetian**, and the fairy-tale castle of **Excalibur**.

Whether you're coming for a weekend or a week, our Top 10 guide is designed to bring together the best of everything the city can offer, from the top **shows** to the hottest **nightclubs**. The guide gives you tips throughout, from **getting married** to shopping for high fashion in the **Forum Shops at Caesars Palace**, plus seven easy-to-follow itineraries that are designed to tie together a clutch of sights in a short space of time. Add inspiring photography and detailed maps, and you've got the essential pocket-sized travel companion. **Enjoy the book, and enjoy Las Vegas.**

Clockwise from top: Caesars Palace, Fremont Street Experience, New York-New York, Grand Canyon, Las Vegas sign, Luxor's sphinx and pyramid, interior of Cosmopolitan

Exploring Las Vegas

The spectacle of the Strip is what makes Las Vegas such a compelling destination, so you can expect to spend most of your time there. Make sure, though, to sample Downtown, where it all began, and see the surrounding deserts. Here are some ideas for two and four days in Las Vegas.

The ARIA Express tram is the best way to reach CityCenter.

Two Days in Las Vegas

Day ❶
MORNING
Kick-start a day on the **Strip** (see pp12–13) with breakfast beside the Grand Canal of **The Venetian** (see pp16–17), before admiring the splendor of **Wynn Las Vegas** (see pp18–19). Then have an alfresco lunch at **Paris Las Vegas** (see p43).
AFTERNOON
Shop under the ever-changing skies of the **Forum Shops at Caesars** (see pp20–21), visit the Conservatory and Botanical Gardens in **Bellagio** (see pp14–15), then ride the free tram to **CityCenter** (see pp24–5). Dine in the **ARIA Resort** (see p25). Stroll past Bellagio's fountains en route to a Cirque du Soleil **show** (see pp58–9).

Day ❷
MORNING
Take a helicopter to **Grand Canyon West** and venture onto the **Skywalk** (see pp30–31). The flight, via the **Hoover Dam** (see pp26–7), gives a real sense of the city's desert setting.
AFTERNOON
Explore **Downtown Las Vegas** (see pp22–3) and discover its past in the **Mob Museum** (see pp92–3). Stay late for the light shows at the **Fremont Street Experience** (see p91).

The Grand Canyon is a spectacular sight of natural beauty, easily accessible from the city.

Key
━ Two-day itinerary
━ Four-day itinerary

New York-New York is a miniature Manhattan, with its own replica Statue of Liberty.

Four Days in Las Vegas

Day ❶
MORNING
Enjoy a coffee in **Jean Philippe Patisserie** (see p69), then visit the **Conservatory and Botanical Gardens** (see p15), both at Bellagio. Ride the free tram to **CityCenter** (see pp24–5).

AFTERNOON
Continue to the miniature Manhattan that is **New York-New York** (see p43), the fairy-tale castle of **Excalibur** (see p43), and the pyramid of the **Luxor** (see p42). Dine in **Mandalay Bay** and stay on for its nightlife.

Day ❷
MORNING
Beat the heat with an early hike at **Red Rock Canyon** (see pp28–9), continue to the **Hoover Dam**, then head back for a buffet lunch in **Caesars Palace** (see p42).

AFTERNOON
Explore Strip highlights, including the flair of **Paris Las Vegas** (see p43), the Renaissance art of **The Venetian**, and the color of **Wynn Las Vegas**. In the evening, catch a Cirque du Soleil **show.**

Day ❸
MORNING
Cut loose on the thrill rides at **Adventuredome** and **Stratosphere Tower** (see pp50–51), or take in the wildlife at **Flamingo Las Vegas** (see p81) and **The Mirage** (see p84).

AFTERNOON
Sample **Downtown Las Vegas**, zooming on the **SlotZilla Zip Line** (see p50) or visiting the **Mob Museum**. See the **Fremont Street Experience** lights.

Day ❹
MORNING
Take either a half-day excursion to **Grand Canyon West**, or a full day at the **South Rim** (see pp30–31).

AFTERNOON
Shop in the **Forum Shops at Caesars**. After a final dinner, take in **Light** nightclub (Wed, Fri & Sat; see p63).

Top 10 Las Vegas Highlights

The atrium of The Forum Shops
at Caesars Palace

TOP10 Las Vegas Highlights

The Entertainment Capital of the World offers just about everything: the world's largest hotels, the brightest stars in show business, shops and restaurants that rival any on earth. It's true, too, that the lights are brighter in Las Vegas. Yet you don't have to go far from the glamour and glitter to find the natural beauty of lakes and the desert as well.

1 The Strip
The neon artery of gambling pulses with excitement. Imaginatively themed resorts make it a street that never sleeps (see pp12–13).

2 Bellagio
The hotel that upped the ante where Las Vegas luxury is concerned is well located, too (see pp14–15).

3 The Venetian
The Italian Renaissance revisited. Minstrels and nobility stroll among Venetian landmarks as gondoliers glide by (see pp16–17).

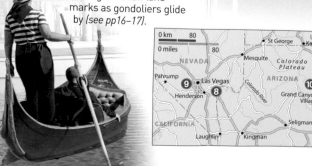

4 Wynn Las Vegas
This opulent mega-resort is set in beautiful landscaped gardens *(see pp18–19)*.

The Forum Shops at Caesars 5
The glory that was Rome provides the backdrop for a choice of upscale shops and restaurants *(see pp20–21)*.

6 Downtown Las Vegas
The city's heart in its early days, it experienced a rebirth in the late 1990s *(see pp22–3)*.

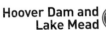

7 CityCenter
This "city-within-a-city" is the most expensive privately funded resort complex in the United States *(see pp24–5)*.

Hoover Dam and Lake Mead 8
An engineering marvel, the dam not only tamed the Colorado River but also created Lake Mead, providing myriad aquatic pursuits, minutes from the city *(see pp26–7)*.

Red Rock Canyon 9
Not far from the city lights, this area provides a welcome getaway from all the glitz *(see pp28–9)*.

10 Grand Canyon
The ultimate excursion from Las Vegas; whether by airplane, bus, or automobile, most visitors say the experience is unforgettable *(see pp30–31)*.

TOP 10 ⭐ The Strip

All the glamour, glitz, and glitter that epitomizes Las Vegas is concentrated along the legendary thoroughfare known simply as the Strip. This 4-mile (6-km) segment of the southern section of Las Vegas Boulevard, sufficiently far from Downtown to be outside the city's official limits, is the epicenter of the global entertainment industry, and home to many of the largest hotels and casinos on the planet. The Strip is a master of reinvention, constantly changing, surprising, and embracing new ways to impress visitors.

The Strip by Night ③

Las Vegas truly comes to life after dark (**right**). Whether you're walking the Strip or soaring above it in a helicopter, that's when you will see the Fountains of Bellagio (see p81) and the Mirage Volcano (see p83) at their most spectacular.

① Shopping

Big-name casinos have showpiece malls – most spectacularly, Caesars Palace has The Forum Shops (see pp20–21) – but there are also stand-alone malls like Fashion Show (see p72) and The Shops at Crystals at CityCenter (see p25).

④ Headliners

Since the unveiling of the Colosseum at Caesars Palace (see p42), Las Vegas has resumed its role as the world's entertainment capital. Regular headliners along the Strip include Celine Dion, Elton John, and Britney Spears.

② Gambling

Gambling is still the bedrock on which Las Vegas rests. Whether you're hoping to beat the bank at baccarat (**below**) or predict the roulette wheel, losing can be surprisingly enjoyable (see pp40–41).

⑤ Fine Dining

The competition between the major casinos to persuade the world's best chefs to open Las Vegas restaurants has turned the city into a foodie's dream. Current highlights are Julian Serrano (see p66), Bouchon Bistro (see p67), Nobu (see p67), and Scarpetta (see p67).

⑥ Themed Architecture

With the Strip's inventive architecture, you can admire the world's great cities, from Paris to New York via Venice, or even time travel to ancient Rome or Egypt (**above**).

7 Shows

Every casino-hotel along the Strip holds at least one theater, each hosting long-running shows that range from long-running hit comedy *Menopause the Musical* via magicians like Penn & Teller to the postmodern antics of the all-conquering Cirque du Soleil **(left)** and the one-of-a-kind Blue Man Group *(see pp58–9)*.

THE MOB

As is vividly portrayed in the 1995 Robert de Niro movie *Casino*, organized crime and Las Vegas were natural bedfellows for several decades from the 1940s. Gangsters were drawn like magpies to the coins piling up effortlessly in so many slot machines. Bugsy Siegel was the trailblazer with his Flamingo Hotel *(see p36)*, while Midwest crime boss Moe Dalitz opened the Desert Inn in 1950. Learn about Las Vegas's connection to the Mob and organized crime at the Mob Museum *(see p92–3)*.

8 Buffets

While cheap-and-cheerful buffets still abound, upscale places like Bellagio *(see pp14–15)* and Wynn Las Vegas *(see pp18–19)* now offer irresistible "gourmet" options, piled with sushi, and other culinary treats.

9 Thrill Rides

A city of thrills of course comes up trumps in thrill rides. The scariest are atop Stratosphere Tower *(see p85)*; others include the Big Apple Coaster at New York-New York **(below)** and the Adventuredome at Circus Circus *(see p52)*.

NEED TO KNOW

MAP M3–R2

General information: Las Vegas Convention and Visitors Authority ▪ 3150 Paradise Rd ▪ 702 892 0711 or 877 847 4858 ▪ www.lasvegas.com

▪ You're on vacation – why *not* have doughnuts for breakfast?! Delicious Krispy Kreme doughnuts are on sale at Excalibur and Circus Circus.

▪ To maximize the excitement, get a hotel room with a view of the Strip. Best of all are The Venetian, Paris, and the rooms in the Luxor pyramid.

▪ Be prepared to shift your body clock later than usual; Las Vegas may keep going around the clock, but the shops are the only places where there's much happening in the morning.

10 Clubbing

Casinos vie to build ever more extraordinary clubs. Leading lights include MARQUEE, TAO Nightclub, and Encore Beach Club *(see pp62–3)*.

Bellagio

From the flower arrangements in the halls to the fixtures in the bathtubs, Bellagio is the epitome of extravagance. The goal of Steve Wynn, who originally conceived this grand monument to leisure, was to create a hotel "that would exemplify absolute quality while emphasizing romance and elegance – romance in the literary sense, a place of ideal beauty and comfort; the world everyone hopes for, as it might be if everything were just right."

① Lobby Ceiling
Visitors are greeted by the dazzling 2,000-sq-ft (186-sq-m) glass sculpture, the *Fiori di Como*, suspended from the lobby ceiling. The creator was Dale Chihuly, the first American artist to be designated a national living treasure. Amazingly, every single flower is different **(left)**.

Via Bellagio ②
You are only likely to frequent Bellagio's shopping promenade if you have deep pockets. The boutiques are as elegant as the Via itself **(right)**, counting among them such names as Prada, Chanel, Armani, and Gucci *(see p72)*.

③ Gallery of Fine Art
Bellagio's art gallery hosts major temporary exhibitions of international artists, past and present, in conjunction with other large art galleries and museums in North America and around the world.

⑤ Theater
Designed for Cirque du Soleil's spectacular water-based production *O (see p58)*, the theater combines old-world magnificence (it is styled after a European opera house) with cutting-edge technology. Central to the production is an impressive 1.5-million-gallon (6.8-million-liter) pool, which can be remodeled to meet each act's needs.

Italianate Theme ④
Fronting a pristine lake with a tree-lined boulevard beyond, this extraordinary resort hotel was built to resemble an idyllic village on the shores of Italy's Lake Como **(right)**. The theme is carried throughout the property – its original 3,000-room tower, the Spa Tower, 19 dining options, and two wedding chapels – creating an atmosphere of opulence.

6 Fountains of Bellagio

Swirling and gyrating with balletic grace, all choreographed to a booming soundtrack that ranges from Beethoven to Broadway, the fountains in Bellagio's 8-acre (3-ha) lake spring to life every half-hour during the afternoon, and every 15 minutes after dark, providing the Strip's finest free show to the crowds that gather on the sidewalk **(below)**.

7 Conservatory and Botanical Gardens

Keen gardeners and plant-lovers will be rewarded with floral displays that change with each season and Chinese New Year. Each change employs the services of no fewer than 140 professionals.

8 Restaurants

Bellagio's superb restaurants include Le Cirque, Michael Mina, Noodles, Jasmine, and Yellowtail. Picasso *(see p66)* has an AAA Five Diamond Award and is decorated with originals.

9 Buffet

The Bellagio Buffet has re-invented the Vegas buffet, eschewing the more common budget bonanza in favour of a tantalizing gourmet spread of quality seafood and meat *(see p70)*.

10 Casino

Less flamboyant and more sophisticated than others, this is the most aesthetically pleasing casino in Las Vegas. Slot-machine carousels are fringed with specially designed fabrics rather than the ubiquitous neon tubing, and the custom-made carpets provide a stylish relief **(right)**.

HIGH ROLLERS

High rollers – gambling's big spenders – are courted by every major casino. Who qualifies (based on the amount he or she bets) varies a good deal, but a really big spender – someone who wagers thousands in an evening – will get superstar treatment from the top hotels. They may get flown to Las Vegas in a private jet, put up in a luxurious suite, and given carte blanche to order whatever they want from the hotel. Like superstars, high rollers are treated with the ultimate discretion, so you may not spot one.

NEED TO KNOW

MAP Q1–2 ■ 3600 Las Vegas Blvd S. ■ 888 987 6667 ■ www.bellagio. com ■ \$\$\$ *(for price categories see p84)*

■ For lunch in a tranquil setting, reserve a table on the terrace at Olives, overlooking Lake Bellagio.

■ For a real treat, indulge yourself with an afternoon spent at the hotel's luxurious spa. Group booking can be arranged for brides and bridesmaids, and there's even a treatment menu specifically for men.

■ To enjoy the best views of Bellagio's fountain show, cross the street and go to the observation level of the Eiffel Tower at Paris Las Vegas *(see p43)*.

🔟 ⭐ The Venetian

Modeled on Venice, Italy, The Venetian is a massive, award-winning property. This all-suite hotel forms a mega-resort with the adjoining Palazzo, and makes an ideal base for exploring the sights of the Strip. The Grand Canal Shoppes, a mall complete with gondolas and singing gondoliers, all set against the backdrop of St. Mark's Square, offers plentiful shopping, and the gaming rooms and lavish spa are also noteworthy. There are also more than 30 fine-dining restaurants and three theaters.

1 Architecture and Ambience
The grandeur of Venice meets Las Vegas glitz, and the results are surprisingly spectacular **(above)**. True, the hotel's Grand Canal is only 1,200-ft (365-m) long as opposed to the original's 2.5 miles (4 km), but any lack of authenticity is more than made up for by the festive Las Vegas ambience.

3 Grand Canal
The Venetian has its very own Wedding Gondola **(above)** to hire for marriage ceremonies. You can even sail under the Rialto Bridge.

4 Grand Colonnade
Reproductions of frescoes framed in 24-karat gold adorn the domed and vaulted ceilings **(left)**. Marble floors, Classical columns, costumed courtiers, and a giant overview of the real Venice all serve to transport the imagination to Italy.

St. Mark's Square 2
So the geography isn't exactly as per the original, but even if you notice you probably won't care – the total effect is extremely aesthetically pleasing, perhaps more so than at any of the other resorts **(right)**.

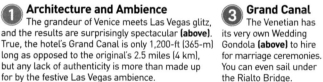

6 The Grand Canal Shoppes at The Venetian

The galaxy of goodies in the shops along the canal (see p73) satisfy a wide range of tastes: there are magic tricks at Houdini's and cookies and cakes at Carlo's Bakery; there is crystal at Swarovski and smart sportswear at Banana Republic. Travel the canal by gondola or meander the walkway linking the stores.

7 Restaurants

Stars of The Venetian's gastronomic line-up include celebrity restauranteur Wolfgang Puck's CUT, Mario Batali's B&B Ristorante, TAO Asian Bistro, and Thomas Keller's Bouchon. Dine alfresco in St. Mark's Square to re-create the Venetian experience.

HIGH HURDLES

The journey of a major hotel-casino from the drawing board to the grand opening is a long and often tortuous process. Of course, plans must be submitted and approved by city government and county commissioners. But the most rigorous scrutiny is reserved not for the building but for those involved in owning and managing the casino. These people are vetted by the Nevada Gaming Commission and subjected to a thorough background check.

8 Canyon Ranch SpaClub

The Venetian's spa has an indoor rock climbing wall, 2 fitness centers, and more than 80 treatment rooms.

5 Nightlife

Spearheaded by the ultra-lavish TAO Nightclub (see p62), along with several resident shows and seven bars and lounges, the Venetian ranks among the Strip's premier nightspots.

9 Casino

Set in the Doge's Palace, the vast casino has 110 table games and 2,000 slot machines. The high rollers' "Renaissance Room" includes replicas of works by Tiepolo, Tintoretto, and Titian. There is a 10,000-sq-ft (929-sq-m) race and sports book on the casino floor, with over 100 seats for personal betting stations.

NEED TO KNOW

MAP P2 ■ 3355 Las Vegas Blvd S.
■ 702 414 1000 or 877 283 6423
■ www.venetian.com ■ $$$ suites only
(for price categories see p84)

■ Splurge on a meal at one of the three Emeril Lagasse restaurants: Delmonico Steakhouse, Table 10, and Lagasse's Stadium.

■ It is almost as much fun – and a lot less expensive – to watch the gondoliers from land as it is to actually ride in the gondolas.

■ If possible, visit The Venetian when there is a full moon and the crowds have thinned: by moonlight it is breathtaking.

10 Madame Tussauds

In a building fashioned after the library on St. Mark's Square, the wax museum opened in 1999 and features well-known celebrities such as Whitney Houston (left). Some say the waxworks here are even more lifelike than those in the London original (see p47).

TOP 10 ⭐ Wynn Las Vegas

Built on the site of the legendary Desert Inn – once owned by billionaire Howard Hughes – this mega-resort was designed to captivate the highest of the high-rollers and the biggest of the big spenders. Over-the-top opulence, from its extravagant villas to exquisite resorts and pools, reigns supreme. Wynn's sister hotel, Encore, is a luxurious addition to the resort, with its own selection of entertainment, restaurants, suites, and shops. The grounds, with an artificial mountain and lake, are spectacular, too.

1 Le Rêve – The Dream

This aquatic masterpiece is the work of director Franco Dragone, who also created shows for Cirque du Soleil. The abstract production features fabulous costumes, jaw-dropping gymnastics, elegant synchronized swimming, and comedy. Shows take place in a theater where the stage is surrounded by a pool (see p59).

3 Casinos

Both the Encore and Wynn casinos seem more intimate than their size would indicate. The gambling stakes are higher than at other casinos, and the casino bars are classy. The decor is lavish, and there's not a flashing light or neon sign in sight. Tile walkways provide natural light and views over the indoor oases (right).

4 Golf Course

Steve Wynn and golfer Tom Fazio collaborated in redesigning this huge course by moving tons of desert sand, repositioning trees, and adding features including the waterfall that players walk under to get from the 18th hole to the traditional-style clubhouse (left).

6 Lake of Dreams

Best viewed from the main staircase in the casino, the extraordinary Lake of Dreams is a surreal sound-and-light show in which ethereal illuminated figures emerge from a mist-shrouded lake (below).

2 Fine Dining

Celebrity restaurants abound at both Wynn and Encore. SW, Wynn's signature steakhouse, is helmed by the innovative David Walzog, while chef Devin Hashimoto creates the freshest Japanese specialties in Mizumi. Wing Lei specializes in serving Chinese flavors with western techniques.

5 XS

This nightclub at Encore is one of the most impressive in the country. Designed to mirror the curves of the human body, it has an undulating golden staircase at the entrance, top-of-the-line production elements, and pyrotechnics. Bottle service is offered on the dance floor and in the poolside cabanas.

7 The Wynn Esplanade

Behind the glass facades of Cartier, Louis Vuitton, Prada, and almost two dozen other upscale stores, lies temptation galore for big winners. Window shoppers can admire the designs and merchandise present at the Esplanade **(left)**.

STEVE WYNN

If any one man can be credited with shaping the Las Vegas Strip, it is Steve Wynn. The creative casino magnate opened the Mirage in 1989 and a new era began – one that impacted on gaming around the world. When he unveiled the Bellagio nine years later, the mega-resort trend was born. He describes his latest creation, Wynn Las Vegas, as "the most expensive, the most complex, the most ambitious structure ever built in the world …"

8 Wedding Salons

For visitors planning to marry here, there are two wedding chapels, the Lavender Salon and the Lilac Salon, with private foyers and bridal rooms. The Primrose Courtyard provides a setting for outdoor weddings under a canopy of trees.

NEED TO KNOW

MAP N2 ■ 3131 Las Vegas Blvd S.
■ 702 770 7100, 888 320 7123 (toll free)
■ www.wynnlasvegas.com ■ $$$ (for price categories see p84)

■ The Buffet features everything from sushi to steak, and is renowned as the finest of the city's "gourmet buffets." There are 15 live cooking stations, and the atmosphere is garden-like with topiaries and pretty foliage. Prices vary depending on the time of visit.

■ Wear walking shoes if you want to explore the resort as there is a lot of ground to cover.

■ Moderately priced fare can be found at Wynn's dining outlets, including Drugstore Café and Terrace Pointe Café. Vegan and vegetarian menus available.

9 Spas

Hotel guests can indulge in a range of wraps, massages, and other treatments. Clients can enjoy them in one of the 45 tranquil treatment rooms, or at the poolside cabana.

10 Encore Beach Club

Epitomizing Las Vegas's new breed of summer-only "day-clubs" – as opposed to nightclubs – the opulent Encore Beach Club **(right)** attracts world-famous celebrities, such as the UK's Prince Harry.

The Forum Shops at Caesars Palace

"So many shops and so little time" is the complaint of most first-time visitors to The Forum Shops. Antiquities, celebrity memorabilia, couturier clothes, and art galleries – there are over 160 stores and restaurants in all. The common areas of the complex are open 24 hours a day, so the savvy visitors who want to window shop and get a close-up view of the fountains and buildings will stroll its lanes in the small hours of the morning.

2 Spiral Escalator
The Forum Shops is home to an impressive freestanding spiral escalator. At three stories high, it is the first of its kind in the United States. It was designed exclusively for the shopping mall by Mitsubishi and added in 2004 after an expansion to the complex (**left**).

3 Sky Ceiling
The domed ceiling simulates a constantly changing sky. The morning sun shines; afternoon clouds float by; evening stars twinkle.

1 Fine Dining
Credit for hosting the Strip's first true fine-dining restaurant, Wolfgang Puck's Spago, goes to the Forum Shops. Still going strong, it has been joined by legendary steakhouse, the Palm; Joe's Seafood, Prime Steak & Stone Crab; Mexican specialists Border Grill; Sushi Roku, a Strip-view sushi bar on Level 3; and several Italian offerings, including Il Molino of New York.

4 Sports Goods
As well as kit for all US team sports, the enormous, multi-level Nike Store at the Atlantis end of the Forum Shops sells replica gear from the big European soccer teams. If you prefer a more classic look, opt instead for a tennis shirt from Lacoste.

6 Architecture
An ancient Roman Forum streetscape is the inspiration behind the design (**above**). The Roman Great Hall is 160 ft (49 m) in diameter and 85 ft (26 m) high. Look for ornate fountains and classic statuary in the central piazzas, and the 50,000-gallon (189,000-liter) saltwater aquarium.

5 Men's Fashion
Many big-name international menswear brands have stores here (**right**). In addition, Tommy Bahama's sells contemporary resort wear, while both Hugo Boss and John Varvatos cater to a more exclusive clientele.

⑧ Women's Fashion

If there's one field in which the mall truly excels, it's women's fashion. You can find almost anything, from Loro Piana's designer boutique to high-street staples such as Gap, Banana Republic, and DKNY **(left)**.

⑦ Casual Dining

As well as more formal restaurants, there are plenty of spots to pause for a quick meal. The two main casual restaurants are huge outlets of The Cheesecake Factory and Planet Hollywood. For a pick-me-up, stop off for an espresso at Ciao Ciao.

⑨ Aquarium

Adjacent to the free, animatronic Atlantis Show, which features pyrotechnic effects, and inside the Forum Shops is the Atlantis Aquarium. More than 150 unique species of tropical fish life can be found in the massive 50,000-gallon saltwater aquarium.

Shoes ⑩

Almost 20 stores are devoted to footwear here. Options range from chic Italian shops specializing in luxury women's shoes, such as Sergio Rossi and Mephisto, to the Western-wear emporium Kemo Sabe – the place for ornate, hand-tooled cowboy boots **(right)**.

COMMERCE OR ENTERTAINMENT?

In most US cities, shopping is an end in itself: go to the mall, make purchases, return home. In Las Vegas, however, shopping has the added dimension of being coupled with entertainment. The Forum Shops and some of the city's other hotels, including Paris Las Vegas and The Venetian, have musicians, singers, mimes, and other performers strolling along the shopping arcades entertaining the crowds. It is all free and adds to the glamour and excitement of Vegas shopping (see pp72–3).

NEED TO KNOW

MAP P1–2 ◾ Caesars Palace, 3500 Las Vegas Blvd S. ◾ 800 634 6001 ◾ Dining reservations 702 731 7731 ◾ www.caesars.com

Shops open 10am–11pm Sun–Thu, 10am–midnight Fri & Sat

◾ Have lunch at one of the restaurants with a sidewalk café, from where you can watch the passing parades.

◾ Visit during the holiday season to admire the elaborate decorations.

◾ If you're visiting with youngsters, arrive early in the morning to avoid the daily rush of shoppers.

◾ Walking from the parking garage to the shops is a shorter trek than through the enormous casino.

TOP 10 ⭐ Downtown Las Vegas

During the 1980s and early 1990s, as the Strip became ever more glamorous, the Downtown area – including the stretch along Fremont Street, formerly known as Glitter Gulch – went further into decline. City fathers and casino owners agreed that something had to be done to reverse the process and took action to see that it was. The resulting efforts have revitalized the area. Development is ongoing, with the opening of new restaurants and attractions offering a greater range of entertainment.

Fremont Street Experience ③

Running from Main St to Fourth St, Fremont Street's most prominent feature is Viva Vision, located near the Plaza Hotel-Casino **(right)**. This is the world's largest graphic display system, containing more than 12.5 million LED lights, which provides spectacular nightly light-and-sound shows every hour from dusk until midnight (see pp90–1).

① Neon Lights

Downtown is home to the city's classic neon lights and signs **(above)**. This is one of the brightest places on earth – so much so that you can stand on the street at midnight and read a newspaper. Even before the Fremont Street Experience was conceived, the country's leading neon designers and engineers were strutting their stuff here.

② Las Vegas's First Casino

The place where it all started is the Sal Sagev Hotel on Fremont Street, now the Golden Gate. Considered Las Vegas's most historic boutique hotel and casino, the original, strange-looking name makes sense in mirror-writing.

④ Signs of the Past

Vegas Vic (see p92) has been waving to passersby on Fremont Street since 1951. More illuminating insights into the history of neon are at the Neon Museum (see p91) at 770 N. Las Vegas Blvd.

⑤ Binion's

Dallas bootlegger and gambler Benny Binion established the property in 1951, and it was owned until 2004 by his descendants **(left)**. The biggest names in poker continue to play here, although the World Series of Poker has moved to Rio (see p102). The hotel-casino is worth a visit to appreciate its old-time atmosphere.

6 SlotZilla Zip Line

The 12-story SlotZilla is the launch point for two separate zip lines, on which riders can either zoom above the crowds sitting up, or fly face-first like Superman **(left)**.

7 Fremont Street Pedestrian Promenade

There is direct access to 10 casinos and more than 60 restaurants from the promenade. Enjoy the vibe of open casinos, where the action spills out onto the streets.

8 Downtown Container Park

Housed in converted shipping containers, this open-air shopping center, on 707 Fremont Street, has boutique shops, bars, restaurants, and galleries. The center also hosts live entertainment and for kids there is an interactive playground with a 33-ft (10-m) high slide and a NEOS play system.

9 Entertainment

In addition to the production shows and lounge acts at most of the hotels, Fremont Street is a center of entertainment and a popular venue for parades and musical performances.

Golden Nugget 10

The four-star Golden Nugget **(right)** is the best-value hotel in the city (rates can fall as low as $59 in the off-season). Its casino is also first-rate (see p39). Try the Chart House for its ambience – and also for a great view of the huge aquarium.

BEGINNINGS

For almost 20 years after its incorporation, entertainment in Las Vegas was simply limited to a few bars and brothels in the red-light district Downtown. The legalization of gambling and arrival of as many as 5,000 dam-construction workers in 1931 changed all that. Casinos opened on Fremont Street, and tourists began to arrive. World War II personnel and their families gave Las Vegas another population surge in the 1940s, and casino building continued apace after the war – as it does to this day.

NEED TO KNOW

MAP J–L4, L3

Golden Gate: 1 Fremont St ■ 702 385 1906

Golden Nugget: 129 Fremont St ■ 702 385 7111

Binion's: 128 Fremont St ■ 702 382 1600

SlotZilla Zip Line: 425 Fremont St ■ 702 678 5780

■ For tasty American fare served alongside stand-out cocktails, try Therapy (518 Fremont St).

■ Most of the action at night in Downtown takes place near Fremont Street Experience.

■ Arrive a few minutes before the hour to see the show at the Fremont Street Experience. Then explore the shops and casinos, or enjoy the stage entertainment.

TOP 10 ⭐ CityCenter

Las Vegas's largest creation is CityCenter, a "city-within-a-city" designed to have everything all in one place. Located on 67 acres (27 ha) at the heart of the Strip, the complex is home to five distinct properties – ARIA Resort, The Shops at Crystals, the Mandarin Oriental, the Vdara Hotel, and the residential Veer Towers. The area also contains a casino, luxury spas, and shops, all within a short distance of each other. At a cost of $8.5 billion, CityCenter is the most expensive privately funded project in the United States.

Architecture ①
Unique architectural features by eight of the world's foremost architects, including Cesar Pelli, abound at CityCenter. Among the highlights is Crystals' quartz-shaped metal-and-glass exterior by Studio Daniel Libeskind **(right)**.

② The Park
Nestled between the Monte Carlo and New York-New York resorts, this dining and entertainment district is a short walk away from CityCenter. There are six restaurants and a T-Mobile Arena, where concerts and sporting events – including home games of the Vegas Golden Knights NHL hockey team – are held.

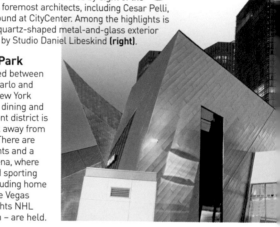

③ ARIA Express
The sleek, free cable-drawn tram that connects the ARIA Resort with the Monte Carlo to the south and Bellagio to the north is an exhilarating vision, straight from some futuristic cityscape **(above)**. A journey offers an interesting vantage point of CityCenter.

NEED TO KNOW

MAP Q1–2 ▪ 3740 Las Vegas Blvd S.

ARIA Resort: 3730 Las Vegas Blvd S., 866 359 7111, $$ (for price categories *see p84*)

The Shops at Crystals: 3720 Las Vegas Blvd S., 866 754 2489

Mandarin Oriental: 3752 Las Vegas Blvd S., 702 590 8888, $$

Vdara Hotel: 2600 W. Harmon Ave, 866 745 7111, $$

▪ Head to Starbucks to start your day with a coffee and a breakfast sandwich, on the mezzanine level of Crystals, near the main entrance by ARIA.

▪ The ARIA Express links CityCenter, Bellagio and Monte Carlo in 3 minutes.

4 Fine Art Collection

There are great permanent displays of fine art throughout CityCenter. Artists such as Maya Lin, Jenny Holzer, Frank Stella, and Richard Long have created pieces ranging from sculptures and paintings to large-scale indoor and outdoor installations.

ECO-FRIENDLY SITE

CityCenter was built with sustainability in mind, and the project has been certified by the US Green Building Council. The ARIA is one of the largest hotels in the world with Leadership in Energy and Environmental Design (LEED) status. Features include natural lighting, an on-site combined heat and power plant, and a recycling program.

7 The Shops at Crystals

Shopping, dining, and entertainment are all found under one roof at this vast retail center. More than 50 designer stores include Tom Ford, Paul Smith, and the largest Louis Vuitton boutique in North America. Various works of art, including a three-story, nest-like Tree House and ice and water sculptures, are dotted throughout **(above)**.

8 Vdara Hotel

This 57-story, all-suite hotel and spa connects to the Bellagio (see pp14–15) and the ARIA via a walkway. Suites boast state-of-the-art technology and full-service kitchens.

9 Dining

Dining options here include restaurants from top chefs, such as Todd English P.U.B. and Wolfgang Puck's Pizzeria & Cucina.

5 Spas

CityCenter spas include the ARIA, with a water garden; the Vdara, offering holistic treatments; and the Mandarin Oriental, where Eastern techniques are used.

6 ARIA Resort

The ARIA Resort **(below)** boasts 4,004 high-tech guest rooms and suites with views of the skyline and surrounding mountains. There are four outdoor pools, 18 restaurants, 7 bars, a spa, and a theater (see p84).

10 Mandarin Oriental

Winner of the Forbes Five-Star Award for hotel, spa, and restaurant, the Mandarin Oriental **(above)** is a 47-story, non-gaming hotel with 392 spacious rooms and suites, and 225 luxury condominiums. Guests check in at the Sky Lobby, and there is a sky bridge to Crystals at CityCenter.

TOP 10 ⭐ Hoover Dam and Lake Mead

Before the construction of the Hoover Dam early last century, the mighty Colorado River often flooded farmland in southern California and Mexico. A series of studies into how to tame the rampaging river led in 1928 to the Boulder Canyon Project Act and the subsequent construction of the dam. This colossus of concrete – a triumph of engineering – not only provides reliable water supplies, flood control, and electricity, but is also a huge tourist attraction, with nearly a million visitors per year.

1 Hoover Dam Visitor Center

Audiovisual and theater presentations as well as multimedia exhibits at the Visitor Center **(below)** explain the processes and perils involved in building this eighth wonder of the modern world. An overlook on top of the center provides a bird's-eye view of the dam, Lake Mead, the Hoover Dam Bridge, and the Black Canyon.

2 Hoover Dam Bridge

Get an unrivaled view of the dam from the Hoover Dam Bridge also known as the Mike O'Callaghan–Pat Tillman Memorial Bridge **(right)**. The sight of 3.2 million cubic yards (2.6 million cubic m) of concrete, standing 727 ft (221 m) high, is truly awe-inspiring.

3 Commercial District, Boulder City

Walk back into 1930s America. The arcaded buildings were the precursors of today's shopping plazas. Boulder Dam Hotel, by contrast, is in Dutch colonial style.

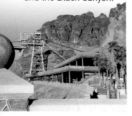

4 Construction Workers' Houses, Boulder City

Up to 8,000 dam workers were housed here, and although many of the buildings have disappeared, cottages 1–12 look much as they did when first built.

5 Lake Mead

The dam's lake is the largest man-made body of water in the US. Its 550 miles (885 km) of shoreline boast canyons and flower-rich meadows; its waters abound with fish. Boulder Beach offers the best swimming.

6 Lake Mead Cruises

The lake's shores come to life seen from the deck of a boat **(below)**. You'll see sandy beaches and rocks of every hue. Look out for burros, jackrabbits, lizards, and bighorn sheep, too.

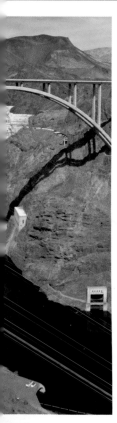

Powerplant and Dam Tours 7

Visitors can descend 530 ft (162 m) for a power-plant tour, or explore the dam's tunnels (right).

8 Scuba Diving

An unusual underwater scene greets divers: in addition to fish, there is a submerged factory where trainloads of gravel for the dam's concrete were cleaned and sorted. Take a trip with a local company; certified divers can rent scuba gear.

9 Hoover Dam Museum, Boulder City

The dam and the people who built it are the focus of this museum, which is housed in the historic Boulder Dam Hotel (see p105, above). Be sure to watch the film chronicling the construction of the dam. Memorabilia, photos, and posters give insights into life in 1930s US.

ANCIENT PEOPLES

Archaeologists disagree about how long humans have lived in the desert along the Colorado River. There were certainly people living downstream from the dam 3,000–4,000 years ago, and possibly as far back as 8,000 years ago. The Patayans were among the first Native Americans known to live in the broader tri-state area (Nevada, Arizona, California), appearing in about AD 900. They lived in brush shelters and ate seeds and plants. Their descendants split into the Hualapai and Mojave tribes.

NEED TO KNOW

MAP T2 ■ 30 miles (50 km) SE of Las Vegas ■ www.usbr.gov/lc/hooverdam

Hoover Dam Visitor Center: Hwy 93, Hoover Dam, Boulder City, NV. 702 494 2517. 9am–4:15pm daily

Tour reservations: 866 730 9097 (toll free)

■ While driving through Boulder City, stock up on drinks and mouthwatering sandwiches at Capriotti's Sandwich Shop (1010 Nevada Highway) to have as a picnic later on a Lake Mead beach.

■ Take a cruise that does not include meals: it will be cheaper and gives you more time to take in the surroundings.

■ Drive along the west shore of Lake Mead to access the Valley of Fire and Lost City Museum (see p111).

10 Black Canyon River Raft Trips

The Colorado River flows lazily below the dam, so rafting (above) is pleasant rather than white-knuckle. It takes a little more than 3 hours to make the 12-mile (19-km) trip to Willow Beach. Look out for petroglyphs carved in the rock, and for ringbolts: before the dam existed, these were used to winch steamboats through Ringbolt Rapids.

TOP 10 ★ Red Rock Canyon

About 225 million years ago, everything at Red Rock Canyon was covered by an inland sea. The escarpment, formations, and caves were created after that sea evaporated, and wind and rain began sculpting the land. This remarkable desert region lies just 24 miles (39 km) from the middle of the Strip. A conservation area since 1990, it is protected from city expansion. The 13-mile (21-km) scenic drive that loops off Highway 159 provides a good overview, but the best way to explore this part of the Mojave Desert is on foot.

③ Red Rock Vista Overlook

The view from this overlook **(right)**, about 1 mile (1.5 km) past the Highway 159 turnoff to the Canyon, is of the Red Rock escarpment, which rises a breathtaking 3,000 ft (1,000 m) from the valley floor. Time your trip to get here at sunrise or sunset when the colors of the sandstone are at their best.

① Hikes and Guided Walks

Of more than 30 miles (50 km) of hiking trails in the canyon **(above)**, the most popular include those to Calico Tanks (featuring red sandstone) and Oak Creek. Guided walks focus on aspects of the environment such as native wildflowers and the area's geology.

② Endangered Desert Tortoises

Look out for brown-shelled tortoises, which, with their lifespan of up to 100 years, may outlive you. They dig burrows in the desert and spend at least 95 per cent of their long lives below ground. Astonishingly, adult tortoises can survive for a year without water.

④ Children's Discovery Trail

At the visitor center, inquire about the *Junior Explorer Discovery Book* and scheduled educational events. Near Willow Springs is the Children's Discovery Trail to Lost Creek. Less than 1 mile (1.5 km) long, it highlights points of interest on the way. The cliffs above it are a good place to spot bighorn sheep.

⑤ Visitor Center

The visitor center **(below)** has area maps, and staff on hand to answer questions. It contains both indoor and outdoor exhibits featuring geological, cultural, and natural history displays.

⑥ Bookstore

The visitor center bookstore covers the local flora, fauna, and geology. Excellent Southwest-themed novels for children and books on local geology, history, and culture are available for purchase.

7 Petroglyphs and Pictographs

The area around Willow Springs contains some fascinating prehistoric rock carvings and paintings **(left)**. The exact meaning of many of the incised and painted symbols is not known, but because the area's early inhabitants were hunters and gatherers, it is believed that many symbolize the procuring of food.

8 Thirteen-Mile Drive

The main scenic loop is a road taking in Rainbow and Bridge mountains, and the Calico Hills. There are stopping points for views along it. Head for Willow Springs for picnics. Most hiking trails are accessible from parking lots on the loop.

9 Tinajas

Prevalent in the Calico Hills and at White Rock Spring, tinajas (or tanks) are naturally formed rock catchments for water. They serve as drinking basins for wildlife and are good places to seek out for photo opportunities.

10 Desert Whiptail Lizards

Common to the western US, these lizards **(below)** have pointed snouts and forked tongues. Recognize them by the four or five light stripes along the back, and the yellow- or cream-colored belly with scattered dark spots.

CYCLING CULTURE

Highway 159, which leads out of Las Vegas toward Red Rock Canyon, is very popular with cyclists, especially on weekend mornings. Use caution when driving on this road. Visitors who want to ride can rent bikes at Las Vegas Cyclery (10575 Discovery Drive), McGhie's (4305 S. Fort Apache Road), and other businesses. Keep an eye out for desert creatures such as jackrabbits and snakes that may dart out onto the road. Take plenty of water and sunscreen.

NEED TO KNOW

MAP T2 ▪ 24 miles (38 km) from mid-Strip

Admission: $7 per vehicle

Campground: $15 per night, per site

Visitor Center: 1000 Scenic Dr. 702 515 5350. 8am–4:30pm daily. www. redrockcanyonlv.org

▪ Stop at a deli or takeout in Las Vegas to pick up a picnic lunch to eat at the Willow Springs picnic area.

▪ Wheelchair users will find plenty of accessible sights to explore near the visitor center and Red Spring boardwalk.

▪ You will need a permit if you want to camp overnight or go rock-climbing at Red Rock Canyon. Apply at the visitor center.

▪ Take the usual precautions when visiting a desert area (see p128).

Grand Canyon

"Overwhelming" and "humbling" are words frequently used to describe the Grand Canyon experience. One of the world's most awesome sights, the canyon is 277 miles (446 km) long, 10 miles (16 km) wide, and as deep as a mile (1.6 km) in places. The canyon encompasses a range of desert and mountain habitats. Day-trippers from Las Vegas usually fly to Grand Canyon West. The more impressive South and North rims lie in the national park, a five-hour drive from the city; best seen with an overnight stay.

1 Skywalk
Jutting out above a fearsome 4,000-ft (1,200-m) abyss at the canyon's less dramatic western end, the horseshoe-shaped, glass-floored Skywalk is the highlight of a day-trip to the Grand Canyon West. You can't take your own camera with you, but don't worry – it's not an experience you're likely to forget (right).

2 Flyovers
Flights over Grand Canyon (below) make for popular day trips from Las Vegas (see p121).

4 Visitor Centers
Information centers at the North and South Rims of the canyon supply free maps as well as *The Guide*, which has general park information; *The Junior Ranger Guide*, listing children's activities; and *The Accessibility Guide*, which has information for disabled visitors. Exhibits and bookstores are located near these centers, as are great observation points too. Ask about evening ranger programs if you plan on spending the night in the park.

3 Tusayan Ruins and Museum
Ruins of rock dwellings inhabited by ancestors of the Hopi Indians around AD 1200 are preserved between South Rim Village and the park's east entrance. The museum has artifacts and exhibits offering an insight into their culture.

5 Whitewater Rafting
Dozens of companies, such as Canyon Explorations (see p121), offer white-water rafting trips along the Colorado River on the canyon floor. Trips vary in length from 6 to 16 days (right).

⑥ Grand Canyon Railway
Vintage train services **(right)** are offered from Williams to the Grand Canyon's South Rim. Vacation packages are also available.

EXPLORATION OF THE CANYON

In 1869, Major John Wesley Powell, a veteran of the American Civil War, led an exploration party along the Colorado River through the canyon. On August 28, three of the men left the group at the rim of Separation Canyon and were killed by Native Americans. Ironically, it was the following day that Powell's expedition emerged safely from the gorge, completing the first exploration of the Grand Canyon.

⑦ Overlooks
Grand views may be found from many canyon overlooks. On the South Rim, Hermit Road hugs the rim west of Grand Canyon Village with nine overlooks. Enjoy great views of the Colorado River far below from Pima Point. Motorists can use Desert View Drive (Hwy 64) along the South Rim east of Grand Canyon Village with spectacular views from Grandview and Moran points, and you can almost see down to Utah from the top of the 70-ft (21-m) Watchtower.

⑧ Hiking Trails
Popular South Rim hikes are the South Kaibab, Bright Angel, and Rim trails *(see p120)*. North Rim hikes include the North Kaibab, Bright Angel Point, and Widforss trails. Don't hike to the canyon floor and back in one day: get an overnight permit.

⑨ California Condors
Standing over 3 ft (1 m) tall and with a wingspan of about 9 ft (3 m), the rare California condor may be spotted flying over the South Rim in summer.

NEED TO KNOW

MAP V2 ■ South Rim 271 miles (436 km), North Rim 255 miles (408 km) E. of Las Vegas ■ Grand Canyon Visitor Center, open 9am–5pm daily, longer hours in summer, 928 638 7888 ■ www.nps.gov/grca ■ Admission charge to enter national park $30 per vehicle or $15 per pedestrian or cyclist

··

■ *See p118* for great places to eat at the Grand Canyon.

■ The South Rim is accessible by road year-round, but the North Rim facilities and road are closed from mid-Oct or Nov to mid-May.

■ You will need a permit to camp outside the official campsites within the national park. Apply in advance at the Backcountry Information Center (www.nps.gov/grca/planyourvisit).

⑩ Grand Canyon West
Grand Canyon West **(above)** is on the Hualapai Indian Reservation near Lake Mead. As well as the Skywalk, it has other viewpoints and native-American-themed attractions.

Following pages Viewpoint over the Grand Canyon

The Top 10 of Everything

**Luminous casino sign
on Fremont Street**

TOP 10 Moments in Las Vegas History

The neon sign outside the Flamingo Hotel and Casino

1 1855: Mormons Establish a Trading Post

Inhabited for centuries by Native Americans and encountered by Spanish explorers in 1829, the Las Vegas area was only permanently settled in 1855 when a group of Mormons, led by Brigham Young, established a trading post here.

2 1931: Gambling Legalized in Nevada

The relaxed gaming laws passed in the Silver State in 1931 encouraged widespread public participation in betting and gambling. In reality, though, both had already been widespread and, in some forms, legal.

3 1935: Boulder Dam Dedicated by Roosevelt

One of the greatest 20th-century hydroelectric projects, the Boulder (later Hoover) Dam was begun in 1931 and completed in 1935, at a human cost of 96 lives (see pp26–7).

4 1940s: Air Conditioning and Irrigation Arrive

The ability of air conditioning and irrigation to keep buildings cool and land green made the Nevada desert far more attractive to developers. In 1941, Los Angeles hotelier Tom Hull bought land 3 miles (5 km) south of Downtown for $150 an acre and built the 100-room El Rancho motel – a new concept in accommodation.

5 Christmas Day, 1946: Bugsy Siegel Opens the Flamingo Hotel and Casino

A handful of hotels and motels followed El Rancho, but only when mobster Benjamin "Bugsy" Siegel built the Flamingo Hotel and Casino was the hitherto Wild West feel of the town replaced with the Miami Beach-style feel that was to become the hallmark of the Strip.

6 1960: The Rat Pack Comes to Town

The extravagant Flamingo was widely imitated in the 1950s, and entertainment was an important part of the new casinos' allure. Frank Sinatra performed at the Sands Hotel in 1960, with friends including John F. Kennedy in the audience. Las Vegas then became a playground of the so-called Rat Pack (Sinatra, Sammy Davis, Jr., Dean Martin, Peter Lawford, Joey Bishop, et al).

The Rat Pack

⑦ 1966: Howard Hughes Arrives

Howard Hughes's Summa Corporation was a dominant player in the Nevada hotel/casino industry. Legend (which makes up much Las Vegas history) has it that the eccentric billionaire arrived in town one day in 1966 by limousine and was whisked up to his suite at the Desert Inn, where he lived as a recluse for several years, with uncut fingernails and hair.

Eccentric billionaire Howard Hughes

⑧ 1990s: The Era of the Theme Hotel Begins

In the 1970s and 1980s, Las Vegas hotels became larger and more flamboyant. In 1991, the ground-breaking MGM Grand, Treasure Island, and pyramid-shaped Luxor launched the theme hotel in earnest.

⑨ 1998: Bellagio Opens

Hotelier Steve Wynn set a new standard for Las Vegas hotels with the luxurious Bellagio (see pp14–15). The former owner of the Mirage hotel group (which he sold to MGM in 2000) is acknowledged as the creative force behind the modern resort concept.

⑩ 2009 Onwards: The New Generation of Resorts

Las Vegas proved its resilience to recession with the unveiling of the futuristic CityCenter neighborhood in 2009, while in 2015, despite filing for bankruptcy, Caesars Entertainment pushed ahead with developments like the LINQ/High Roller complex.

TOP 10 FAMOUS RESIDENTS

Silent-film star Clara Bow

1 Clara Bow
Silent-film star Clara Bow, who became known as the "It Girl," lived in Las Vegas with her actor husband Rex Bell.

2 Jerry Lewis
The comedian who famously teamed up with singer Dean Martin performed in Las Vegas for many years.

3 Howard Hughes
The eccentric billionaire used his inheritance to make still more money in the film and airline industries before becoming a force in gambling.

4 Liberace
Wladziu Valentino Liberace – aka "Mr. Show Business" – first opened at the legendary (now closed) Riviera in 1955.

5 Wayne Newton
In 1957, 15-year-old entertainer Wayne Newton started his career at the Fremont casino; he is still frequently seen at events in the city.

6 André Agassi
Born in Las Vegas in 1970, Agassi rose to become one of the world's greatest (and most popular) tennis players.

7 Debbie Reynolds
The film star was also the owner of a hotel-casino and a museum of Hollywood memorabilia.

8 Robert Goulet
The actor/entertainer was a veteran of such hit Broadway musicals as *Carousel* and *Man of La Mancha*.

9 Siegfried & Roy
These German magicians are among the city's best-known residents.

10 Phyllis McGuire
The entertainer is fondly remembered as one third of the singing McGuire Sisters, whose hits included "Sincerely."

TOP 10 Casinos

1 Plaza Hotel and Casino

Housed in the former railway station of Las Vegas, facing directly along Fremont Street, the enormous Plaza Hotel and Casino has reinvented itself in recent years to provide once again the quintessential Downtown gambling experience, which is much less slick than what you will find on the Strip. Sports betting has been on offer here for longer than at any other casino in the city, and now also includes a Race and Sports Book run by William Hill *(see p93)*.

2 Monte Carlo

MAP Q1–2 ▪ 3770 Las Vegas Blvd S. ▪ 702 730 7777 ▪ www.montecarlo.com

The building reflects its European namesake, but the casino is typically Vegas, with the usual machines and table games. Its slot club is, however, superior to most, and the air seems fresher than in most casinos, too.

3 El Cortez

MAP K4 ▪ 600 E. Fremont St ▪ 702 385 5200 ▪ www.elcortezhotelcasino.com

The definitive Downtown casino, a short walk east of the roofed

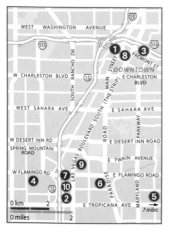

and pedestrianized blocks of Fremont Street, is renowned for the low odds on its gaming tables and its (relatively) high-paying slot machines. If you like your gambling hard-bitten, this is the place to come. Five per cent free play is offered with ATM withdrawals of over 200 dollars.

The casino floor at the Palms

4 The Palms

MAP B4 ▪ 4321 W. Flamingo Rd ▪ 702 942 7777 ▪ www.palms.com

Aimed, unusually, at hip out-of-town clubbers and budget-conscious locals alike, the Palms offers a winning combination of good-value gambling and a glamorous setting. Hoping to lure gamblers the half-mile away from the Strip, it vigorously promotes itself as having the "loosest" (best-paying) slot machines in Las Vegas, while high rollers too relish its partying, big-spending weekend vibe.

5 Sunset Station

Primarily patronized by local residents, Sunset Station is located just across from the Galleria at Sunset shopping mall. The casino benefits from plenty of natural light and is well ventilated, too. It also has a Kids' Quest (nursery), where regular play events, with themes such as Superheroes and Comic Capers, are run *(see p102)*.

6 Hard Rock Hotel
MAP Q3 ▪ 4455 Paradise Rd
▪ 702 693 5000 ▪ www.
hardrockhotel.com

Out on its own, situated a mile to the east of the Strip, the Hard Rock is a destination resort for those – predominantly Californians – who enjoy casino gambling as part of an all-round rock'n'roll lifestyle of partying, clubbing, and big-name gigs. It even offers swim-up blackjack and craps tables, set in the swimming pool and staffed by bikini-clad dealers.

7 Bellagio
Ranking among the plushest of all the major Strip casinos, Bellagio offers as swanky a gaming experience as you could ever hope to find. There are exclusive baccarat and poker areas reserved for high rollers, and video games inlaid into the marble counters. It is a great place to take advantage of the Las Vegas custom whereby active gamblers are plied with free drinks (see pp14–15).

8 Golden Nugget
MAP K4 ▪ 129 E. Fremont St
▪ 800 846 5336 ▪ www.
goldennugget.com

This casino sets itself apart from its Downtown neighbors, in terms of both its clientele and its ambience. The restaurants are very good, and the casino is a pleasant place to gamble while waiting to see the Fremont Street Experience (see p91), which takes place just outside the doors of the complex.

Harrah's casino sign

9 Harrah's
MAP P2 ▪ 3475 Las Vegas Blvd S. ▪ 702 369 5000
▪ www.harrahs.com

One of the most respected names in the gaming industry, Caesars has more than a dozen properties across the US, and this one in particular offers value for money in service, food, and ambience. Harrah's has one of the best player's clubs as far as prizes are concerned. The club card can be used at any Caesars property.

10 The Cosmopolitan
MAP Q2 ▪ 3708 Las Vegas Blvd S. ▪ 702 698 7000
▪ www.cosmopolitanlasvegas.com

There is no more electrifying and energizing casino in Las Vegas than the vibrant, buzzing Cosmopolitan – especially late on a weekend evening, when its clubs and bars are packed to bursting point. Unlike its corporately owned neighbors, The Cosmopolitan does its utmost to prevent anyone leaving, and the big-game atmosphere in its Race and Sports Book is unbeatable.

The vibrant Cosmopolitan

TOP 10 Gambling in Las Vegas

"Progressive" slot machines, with their shared jackpot rising

1 Slot Machines

While today's slot machines are sophisticated computers, rather than one-armed bandits, the principle is the same as ever. The casinos offer a payback of 85–95 per cent, but the hope of a jackpot keeps gamblers playing. On "progressive" machines, which are linked across Nevada by microchip, the progressive jackpot grows rapidly, as every player in the state contributes to it.

2 Blackjack

In blackjack – also known as "pontoon" – each player is dealt two cards, then tries to create a hand adding nearly, or exactly, to 21. The aim is also to beat the dealer, who builds his own hand following fixed rules. There is a "correct" strategy for every situation, but the system is hard to learn.

3 Poker

Most poker players in Las Vegas play either Seven-Card Stud or Texas Hold 'Em, and thus compete against whoever is seated at the same table – so beware, you may be playing with experts. If you would

Caesars Palace poker chip

rather play against the casino, choose a format like Let It Ride or Pai Gow Poker.

4 Wheel of Fortune

This sideshow game is designed to lure in passing non-gamblers. The dealer spins a large wheel that is divided into segments marked with different dollar amounts. When the wheel stops, an arrow indicates the winning segment. For each dollar you bet on that amount, you win that many dollars. The odds, though, are poor.

5 Roulette

The classic game of pure chance, roulette lets players bet on which slot in a numbered, spinning wheel a dropped ball will land on. For the best odds, look for a wheel that holds just one "0," and not, like most in Las Vegas, a "00" slot as well.

6 Video Poker

Video poker is Five-Card Draw poker played on the screen of a slot machine rather than against real-life opponents. Many gamblers find it addictive, partly because on certain machines, following a perfect strategy gives you better odds than the casino.

7 Baccarat

Baccarat is a quick-fire card game requiring no skill and offering (relatively) good odds. Most casinos only offer it to big-stakes gamblers – and it's from baccarat-loving high-rollers that they rake in almost half of their table-gaming revenue.

8 Sports Betting

Not only is Nevada rare for the US in offering legal sports betting, but free drinks are also served to those gambling here. Small wonder that the "Race and Sports Book" in each casino is usually packed, with a party atmosphere for major events.

9 Keno

Keno is a bingo-like game; each player chooses up to twenty numbers between 1 and 80. Match five or more of the twenty drawn by the casino, and you win small; match all twenty and you win big.

Craps players at Golden Nugget

10 Craps

More than any other casino game, craps feels like a team game; players cluster excitedly around the high-walled table to whoop and roar as one throws the dice and the rest lay their bets. Take a free lesson if you don't know the rules – you could never learn by watching.

TOP 10 CASINOS FOR FREE GAMBLING LESSONS

Circus Circus sign

1 Circus Circus
Daily lessons are: blackjack at 10:30am; roulette at 11:30am; craps at 10:30am Wed, 11:30am Fri–Sat (see p85).

2 The D
MAP C3 ▪ 301 E. Fremont St
▪ www.thed.com
Texas Hold 'Em lessons are at 10am; roulette at 11am; craps at noon daily.

3 Excalibur
Daily lessons are: poker at 11am; roulette at 11am and 7pm; blackjack at 11:30am and 7:30pm; and craps at 12:30pm and 8pm (see p43).

4 Golden Nugget
Daily lessons are: poker and craps at 10am; Pai Gow Poker at 10:30am; roulette at 11:30am; and blackjack at noon (see p39).

5 Luxor
Poker lessons are at 10am; craps, roulette, and blackjack lessons are at noon daily (see p42).

6 MGM Grand
MAP C4 ▪ 3799 Las Vegas Blvd S.
▪ www.mgmgrand.com
Daily Poker lessons are at 10:30am, 6pm.

7 Monte Carlo
Craps lessons are at 11am daily (see p38).

8 Stratosphere
Poker lessons are held at 8am on weekend mornings (see p85).

9 South Point
MAP C5 ▪ 9777 Las Vegas Blvd S.
▪ www.southpointcasino.com
Craps lessons are held at 10:15am Tue and Thu and 11:15am Sat.

10 The Venetian
Lessons are Sun–Fri: craps at 11am & 7pm (Sat 11am only); blackjack at 11:30am & 7:30pm (Sat 11:30am only) (see pp16–17).

TOP 10 Theme Hotels

③ Caesars Palace

MAP P1–2 ▪ 3570 Las Vegas Blvd S. ▪ 800 634 6001 ▪ www.caesarspalace.com ▪ $$

Caesars Palace opened in 1966 and was long the Strip's most opulent and most ostentatious hotel. Fifty years on, Caesars continues to spend millions updating its ancient-Roman theme to keep up with newcomers. The cocktail goddesses still wear toga-like costumes, and Cleopatra's Barge (a floating lounge) is still here too, but the entire Strip frontage has become an open-air plaza, dominated by the vast Colosseum, which plays host to performers like Celine Dion and Elton John.

① The Venetian

Whether or not The Venetian really evokes accurate images of Venice is beside the point: the sum of the hotel's parts adds up to an aesthetically pleasing whole (see pp16–17).

② Luxor

MAP R1 ▪ Luxor Hotel and Casino, 3900 Las Vegas Blvd S. ▪ 702 262 4444 ▪ www.luxor.com ▪ $

One of the most distinctive buildings on the Strip, Luxor's 30-floor pyramid fronted by a giant sphinx sets the tone of this resort. Inside is a replica of the Great Temple of Ramesses II and tiered stories that lead to the top of the pyramid.

④ Bellagio

Although the elegant Bellagio casino is modeled on the real-life village of Bellagio, set on the coast of Lake Como in northern Italy, its decor is more generally intended to evoke the *belle époque* opulence of Europe in the years before World War I began, with its overall grandeur designed to evoke, and indeed surpass, legendary European hotels of the era, such as the Ritz Paris. Be sure not to miss seeing the Roman gardens, which are situated just behind the check-in desk (see pp14–15).

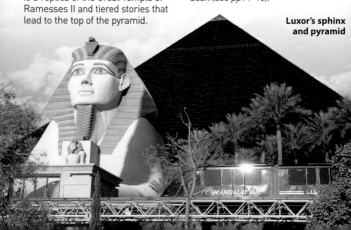

Luxor's sphinx and pyramid

Statue of Liberty, New York-New York

dining and nightlife options attract a trendy crowd. There is also a spa, two swimming pools, and a 6,700-seat theater.

(5) **New York–New York**
MAP R1–2 ▪ 3790 Las Vegas Blvd S. ▪ 800 689 1797 ▪ www.newyorknewyork.com ▪ $
The Statue of Liberty raises her torch over the busiest intersection in Las Vegas. Nearby, the Empire State, CBS, and Chrysler Buildings rub shoulders with the Brooklyn Bridge, Grand Central Station, and the New York Public Library. New York-New York is an exciting place to stay, with all manner of well-observed details throughout.

(6) **Hard Rock Hotel**
The huge guitar sign outside and an enormous chandelier with saxophone pendants clearly identify this as a Hard Rock enterprise. Throughout the public rooms are displays of rock-and-roll memorabilia. And you'll hear only one kind of piped music, of course. There is live music from rock bands most evenings and pool parties with DJs during the day (see p39).

(7) **Planet Hollywood**
MAP Q2 ▪ 3667 Las Vegas Blvd S. ▪ 866 919 7472 ▪ www.caesars.com/planet-hollywood ▪ $
Las Vegas goes Hollywood at this stunningly modern resort and casino conveniently located near the center of the Strip. The 2,567 movie-themed rooms will appeal to cinema fans, while the vibrant

(8) **Paris Las Vegas**
MAP Q2 ▪ 3655 Las Vegas Blvd S. ▪ 702 946 7000 ▪ www.caesars.com/paris-las-vegas ▪ $
Alas, the City of Light has to lose something in translation to the City of Bright Lights. Even so, the Eiffel Tower model is impressive; the bicycle-riding delivery boy and a cheery "Bonjour" from valet-parking attendants are nice touches, too.

(9) **Circus Circus**
As its name suggests, this hotel-casino contains the world's largest permanent circus, as well as an indoor, 5-acre (2-ha) theme park (see p81).

Indoor theme park at Circus Circus

(10) **Excalibur**
MAP R1–2 ▪ 3850 Las Vegas Blvd S. ▪ 702 597 7777 ▪ www.excalibur.com ▪ $
One of the first theme hotels (built in 1990), this is still a favorite, and a big hit with children. The legend of King Arthur and his Knights is the theme that runs through the games arcade and continues into the "Canterbury Wedding Chapel."

For a key to hotel price ranges see p84

TOP10 Wedding Chapels

1 Viva Las Vegas
MAP L3 ■ 1205 Las Vegas Blvd S. ■ 702 384 0771

This chapel is known for its Elvis-themed and traditional weddings, as well as ceremonies set against backdrops such as the Red Rock Canyon. Stars like Angelina Jolie and Matt LeBlanc have made appearances here.

2 Bellagio Wedding Chapels
MAP Q1–2 ■ Bellagio, 3600 Las Vegas Blvd S. ■ 702 693 7700, 888 987 3344

Bellagio's two chapels provide some of the most elegant and romantic wedding venues in Las Vegas. Both have a stained-glass window behind the altar, while ornate lamps and chandeliers of amethyst and Venetian glass complement the pastel shades of the furnishings. Personalized services are available, as well as both wedding and reception planning.

Elegant wedding chapel at Bellagio

3 Little Church of the West
MAP C5 ■ 4617 Las Vegas Blvd S. ■ 702 739 7971

The Little Church of the West opened in 1942, making it the oldest wedding chapel in Las Vegas. It is a favorite with the stars: Zsa Zsa Gabor and George Sanders, Angelina Jolie and Billy Bob Thornton, and Cindy Crawford and Richard Gere have all graced its aisle.

4 Jewish Temples
Temple Beth Sholom (Conservative United), 10700 Havenwood Ln ■ 702 804 1333

There are very few churches and synagogues – as distinct from wedding chapels – that perform "walk-in" ceremonies. Marriage requirements vary from congregation to congregation. Contact Temple Beth Sholom for further information.

5 Christ Church Episcopal
MAP M4 ■ 2000 S. Maryland Parkway ■ 702 735 7655

This traditional Episcopal church is the closest one to the Strip. Bear in mind that churches in the Episcopal Diocese of Nevada require couples to attend prenuptial meetings with the rector of the church before a wedding can be performed.

6 Chapel of the Flowers
MAP L3 ■ 1717 Las Vegas Blvd S. ■ 702 735 4331

Of the three separate chapels in this picturesque little ensemble, the Victorian Chapel is the most popular with couples seeking a touch of tradition. There is also a waterfall and a "glass garden" adorned with illuminated glass flowers.

Indoor wedding salon at Wynn

7 Wedding Salons at Wynn

MAP N2 ■ Wynn Las Vegas, 3131 Las Vegas Blvd S. ■ 702 770 7400

Wynn Las Vegas has three wedding salons to choose from – two are indoors and one is outdoors. For couples hoping to ease the stress of the big day, seven all-inclusive wedding packages are available, ranging from the simple to the over-the-top opulent.

8 Canterbury Wedding Chapels

MAP R1–2 ■ Excalibur, 3850 Las Vegas Blvd S. ■ 702 597 7278

Create your own version of Camelot by marrying your knight in shining armor in one of Excalibur's two medieval-style chapels. For those seeking a truly historic-themed wedding, don't be deterred if you don't have a ball gown or suit of armor; a variety of costumes for both men and women are available for rent. Vow-renewal services are also on offer for the already-wed.

9 Sundance Helicopters

MAP C5 ■ 5596 Haven St ■ 702 736 0606 or 800 653 1881

For a truly unforgettable wedding day, Sundance Helicopters offers this all-inclusive package. A stretch limousine whisks you to a private helicopter that carries you to Grand Canyon West for a marriage ceremony overlooking the Colorado River, before flying you back over the Strip.

10 A Little White Wedding Chapel

MAP L4 ■ 1301 Las Vegas Blvd S. ■ 702 382 5943

This wedding chapel represents what for many people is the epitome of Las Vegas; it has acquired a reputation for hosting rather unusual weddings. It was here in the spring of 2001 that a mass wedding took place, officiated by multiple Elvises. And for the bride and groom who are acting on impulse or whose hectic lives leave them with only a few minutes to spare, the Little White Wedding Chapel offers a drive-through wedding window, where they can exchange vows without leaving the front seat of their car. The window never closes, and no appointment is necessary.

The drive-through wedding window at A Little White Wedding Chapel

🔟 Museums and Galleries

1 Luxor Exhibits

MAP R1 ▪ Luxor, 3900 Las Vegas Blvd S. ▪ 702 262 4400 ▪ Open 10am–10pm daily ▪ www.rmstitanic.net; www.bodiestheexhibition.com ▪ Admission charge

The Luxor pyramid's upper level holds two fascinating permanent displays. *Titanic: The Artifact Exhibition* tells the story of the ill-fated liner, and preserves items recovered from the wreck, while *Bodies: The Exhibition* is a gruesome but gripping gallery of plastinated human corpses.

2 Atomic Testing Museum

MAP Q4 ▪ 755 E. Flamingo Rd ▪ 702 794 5151 ▪ Open 10am–5pm Mon–Sat, noon–5pm Sun ▪ www.nationalatomictestingmuseum.org ▪ Admission charge

Nevada was the leading nuclear-testing facility in the US from 1951 to 1992, and this museum tells the history of the Atomic Era with artifacts and recreations from the Cold War period. The Ground Zero Theater is a bunker replica that shows visitors a film of an atomic explosion, accompanied by sounds, hot air, and vibrations. Las Vegas's weather station is located outside.

3 Nevada State Museum and Historical Society

MAP C3 ▪ 309 S. Valley View Blvd, at the Springs Preserve ▪ 702 486 5205 ▪ Open 9am–5pm Tue–Sun ▪ www.springspreserve.org ▪ Admission charge

This museum has a collection that includes specimens from Nevada mines, preserved Nevada wildlife, Las Vegas showgirl costumes, and a $25,000 chip from the Dunes hotel.

4 Las Vegas Natural History Museum

MAP J5 ▪ 900 Las Vegas Blvd N. ▪ 702 384 3466 ▪ Open 9am–4pm daily ▪ www.lvnhm.org ▪ Admission charge

Highlights include the international wildlife room, a children's hands-on exploration room, and a marine-life gallery. The Treasures of Egypt exhibit features reproduced artifacts of ancient Egyptian life.

Dinosaur, Natural History Museum

5 Bellagio Gallery of Fine Art

MAP Q1–2 ▪ Bellagio, 3600 Las Vegas Blvd S. ▪ 877 957 9777 ▪ Open 10am–8pm daily ▪ www.bellagio.com ▪ Admission charge

This world-class gallery presents temporary exhibitions of 19th- and 20th-century artworks and objects drawn from international collections.

A machine gun on display at The Mob Museum

6 The Mob Museum
MAP J4 ▪ 307 Stewart Ave
▪ 702 229 2734 ▪ Open 9am–9pm
daily ▪ www.themobmuseum.org
▪ Admission charge

Set in the Downtown courthouse that once hosted Senate hearings into organized crime, this lively, exhaustive museum traces the decades-long entanglement between Las Vegas and mobsters, gangsters, and G-men. A café, brewery, and distillery are due to open in late 2017.

7 Clark County Museum
MAP G6 ▪ 1830 S. Boulder Hwy, Henderson ▪ 702 455 7955 ▪ Open 9am–4:30pm daily ▪ Admission charge

This unusual museum showcases historic buildings that have been relocated from around the state, as well as contemporary local artifacts.

8 Las Vegas Springs Preserve
MAP C3 ▪ 333 S. Valley View Blvd ▪ 702 822 7700
▪ Open 9am–5pm daily ▪ www.springs preserve.org ▪ Admission charge

The Springs Preserve explores the history of Las Vegas through exhibits, botanical gardens, hiking trails, animal shows, galleries, classes, and events for the whole family.

9 The Neon Museum
MAP D2–3 ▪ 770 Las Vegas Blvd N. ▪ 702 387 6366 ▪ Tours by appointment only – call or book on website ▪ www.neonmuseum.org ▪ Admission charge

Here, neon signs are considered a form of art. The museum has on display a fascinating and eclectic collection of outdoor signage that casts an illuminating glow on Las Vegas history. The signs date from the 1930s to the present day.

Display at The Neon Museum

10 Madame Tussauds
MAP P2 ▪ The Venetian, 3377 Las Vegas Blvd S. ▪ 702 862 7800 ▪ Open 10am–9pm Sun–Thu, 10am–10pm Fri–Sat ▪ www.madame tussauds.com/LasVegas ▪ Admission charge

Get up close to your favorite celebrity at this branch of the famous waxwork museum. For authenticity, many items of clothing and props used in the exhibitions have been purchased at celebrity auctions.

Following pages The Venetian's canal

🔟 Thrill Rides and Simulators

The Canyon Blaster roller coaster at Adventuredome

1 Adventuredome
MAP M–N2 ■ Circus Circus, 2880 Las Vegas Blvd S. ■ 702 794 3939 ■ Open daily, hours vary ■ Admission charge

There are several fun rides to sample at Adventuredome, Circus Circus' indoor theme park. Possibly the most exciting ride is the high-speed Canyon Blaster, which is billed as "the only double-loop, double-corkscrew indoor roller coaster." Disk'O is a rocking and spinning ride accompanied by loud disco music.

2 Big Shot
MAP L–M3 ■ Stratosphere Tower, 2000 Las Vegas Blvd S.

Located on the world's tallest observation tower, the Big Shot shoots riders 160 ft (50 m) into the air. They then free-fall back to the launchpad. It's not a ride for the faint hearted, or for kids. Ride at night for a great view of the Strip.

3 The Desperado
MAP T2 ■ Buffalo Bill's, 31900 Las Vegas Blvd S., Primm Valley, 35 miles (56 km) south of Las Vegas on I-5 ■ 702 386 7867 ■ Height restrictions

Billed as one of the fastest roller coasters in the US, the Desperado reaches speeds of up to 80 mph (129 kph). Try to catch the great views of the Primm Valley from the highest point. If that is too daring for you, try the Frog Hopper, a ride that simulates a leaping frog, or get drenched on the Adventure Canyon Log Flume.

4 SlotZilla Zip Line
MAP K4 ■ Fremont St

This colossal slot machine launches two tiers of riders – some lying prone in harnesses, others seated – to fly beneath the canopy of Downtown's Fremont Street Experience.

(5) Airline Captain for a Day
MAP E5 ■ 1771 Whitney Mesa Dr., Henderson ■ 702 529 4806

Take control of a full motion flight simulator and feel what it's like to pilot a real Boeing 737. This 30-minute experience takes place in the same simulators where pilots train.

(6) SkyJump Las Vegas
MAP L–M3 ■ Stratosphere Tower, 2000 Las Vegas Blvd S. ■ 702 380 7777 ■ Age restrictions

This "controlled free fall" lets brave souls jump 855 ft (261 m) from the 108th floor of the Stratosphere to a landing mat. Jumpers reach 40 mph (64 kph) as they soar through the air before landing with their feet back on the ground. Purchase a package deal to jump both at night and during the day.

(7) The Big Apple Coaster
MAP R1–2 ■ New York–New York, 3790 Las Vegas Blvd S.

For those more thrill-seeking riders who dare to keep their eyes open during this white-knuckler, the Coney Island-style ride offers spectacular views of the Strip. The coaster route writhes, dips, dives, and loops around the resort's perimeter. While riding, you'll drop 144 ft (44 m) and hit speeds of 67 mph (108 kph).

The Big Apple Coaster

High Roller above The LINQ fountains

(8) High Roller
MAP P2 ■ The LINQ, 3535 Las Vegas Blvd S.

One of the world's biggest observation wheels, the High Roller stands at a height of 550 ft (168 m) and is located at the heart of the Strip. It provides fantastic views of the city from the top.

(9) Vegas Indoor Skydiving
MAP N3 ■ 200 Convention Center Drive ■ 702 731 4768

Vegas Indoor Skydiving advises potential customers that skydiving is not without risk, but this is a great place to gain wings without the use of an airplane or a para-chute. The one-hour experience includes training and a simulated skydive in a vertical wind tunnel complete with a mesh trampoline wall and foam-padded walls.

(10) Richard Petty Driving Experience
MAP E1 ■ Las Vegas Motor Speedway, 7000 Las Vegas Blvd N. ■ 800 237 3889

After instruction, participants can get into the driver's seat of an authentic NASCAR-style stock car, and go, go, go! Even if you can't drive, a passenger-seat ride is also available.

TOP 10 Children's Attractions

1 Adventuredome

This indoor amusement park in the Circus Circus resort has an extensive array of rides and games designed to keep kids as well as adults entertained for hours. They can ride the Canyon Blaster, a looping roller coaster, or the Drifters, a Ferris wheel that simulates a hot-air balloon. Riders should expect plenty of twists and drops on the El Loco roller coaster *(see p50)*.

El Loco roller coaster, Adventuredome

2 SoBe Ice Arena

MAP B2 ■ Fiesta Rancho Casino Hotel, 2400 N. Rancho Drive ■ 702 631 7000 ■ Open daily, hours vary ■ Admission charge

This NHL-regulation-sized rink offers both figure skating and ice hockey facilities, as well as skate rental and lessons.

3 Siegfried & Roy's Secret Garden and Dolphin Habitat

MAP P1–2 ■ The Mirage, 3400 Las Vegas Blvd S. ■ 702 791 7111 ■ Open 10am–7pm daily ■ Admission charge

These two attractions come as a package, combining education and entertainment. Watch the dolphins from above then use the tunnel for underwater viewing. The Secret Garden is an oasis of trees and greenery, with residents including white tigers, panthers, leopards, and rare white lions.

4 Fun Dungeon

MAP R1–2 ■ Excalibur, 3850 Las Vegas Blvd S. ■ Open 10am–10pm daily

Located on the lower level of the Excalibur hotel and casino, this collection of over 200 rides and games includes several old classics, as well as new, high-tech video games. The arcade offers 15 carnival midways, 106 prize redemption games, 10 sports games, and 60 arcade games, such as the Mega Stacker, Big Bass, and Key Master.

7 Shark Reef Aquarium

MAP R1–2 ■ Mandalay Bay, 3950 Las Vegas Blvd S. ■ 702 632 7777 ■ Open 10am–8pm Sun–Thu, 10am–10pm Fri–Sat (May 24–Sep 1: 10am–10pm daily) ■ Admission charge

North America's only predator-based aquarium has more than 2,000 animals in 1.6 million gallons million litres) of water. Over 100 sharks, as well as giant rays, piranha, jellyfish, and sawfish surround visitors as they walk through an underwater glass tunnel.

Display in CSI: The Experience

among flamingoes, swans, ducks, turtles, pelicans, and koi in this quiet escape from the hectic Strip. There are feeding presentations at the island daily at 8:30am and 2pm.

8 Las Vegas Mini Gran Prix

MAP A2 ■ 1401 N. Rainbow Blvd ■ 702 259 7000 ■ Open 10am–10pm Sun–Thu, 10am–11pm Fri–Sat ■ Admission charge

Adult Gran Prix cars, sprint karts, go-karts, kiddie karts, plus the Dragon Coaster, Super Slide, and lots of arcade games make this a favorite off-Strip destination for Las Vegas kids as well as visitors.

6 CSI: The Experience

MAP R2 ■ MGM Grand, 3799 Las Vegas Blvd S. ■ 702 891 5749 ■ Open 9am–9pm daily ■ Admission charge

Older children will enjoy the chance to turn real-life detective, following the forensic clues to solve one of the three intricate murder mysteries in this interactive attraction. First comes a meticulous examination of the crime scene; then the lab, where characters from the TV series *CSI* offer on-screen guidance.

9 DISCOVERY Children's Museum

MAP K3 ■ Donald W. Reynolds Discovery Center, 360 Promenade Place ■ 702 382 5437 ■ Open Jun–Aug: 10am–5pm Mon–Sat, noon–5pm Sun; Sep–May: 9am–4pm Tue–Fri, 10am–5pm Sat, noon–5pm Sun ■ Admission charge

West of Downtown, this museum features 58,000 sq ft (5,388 sq m) of educational play. Its centerpiece, the 60-ft (18-m) Summit Tower, is filled with hands-on science exhibits.

7 Flamingo Wildlife Habitat

MAP P2 ■ Flamingo Las Vegas, 3555 Las Vegas Blvd S. ■ 702 733 3349 ■ Open dawn–dusk daily

Step through the doors and you'll be transported to a place of lush foliage, exotic birds, and other animals. The creatures all live on islands and in streams surrounded by stunning landscape and waterfalls, and are cared for by a team of experts. Walk

10 Red Rock Lanes

MAP A3 ■ Red Rock Resort, 11011 W. Charleston Avenue ■ 702 797 7777 ■ Open 8am–2am daily ■ Admission charge

This 72-lane bowling center comes equipped with a great sound system, lighting effects, fog machines, image generators, and disco balls to turn an ordinary afternoon into a party.

A bowler at Red Rock Lanes

TOP 10 Golf Courses

3,053 ft (930 m). The location provides stunning panoramic views of the Strip *(see pp12–13)*, and the impressive layout has bunkers, water hazards, rolling terrain, and narrow fairways, which add to the challenge this course offers.

3 DragonRidge Country Club

MAP E6 ■ 552 S. Stephanie St, Henderson ■ 702 614 4444

With its manicured fairways, bent-grass greens, and dramatic elevation changes, DragonRidge offers some of the most spectacular views in the valley. The course is private, with limited public play.

1 Spanish Trail Golf Club

MAP A5 ■ 5050 Spanish Trail Ln ■ 702 364 5050

Designed by Robert Trent Jones, Jr., this club offers three individual nines that can be played in three different 18-hole combinations. The 27 holes at the club offer fast, undulating greens and tree-lined fairways. The appropriately named Lakes Course has water coming into play on six of its nine holes.

2 Highland Falls at Golf Summerlin

10201 Sun City Blvd ■ 702 254 7010

Former Masters winner Billy Casper designed this course, which at its highest reaches an elevation of

4 Angel Park Golf Club

MAP A3 ■ 100 S. Rampart Blvd ■ 702 254 4653

The Palm and the Mountain, this club's two 18-hole championship layouts designed by the legendary American golfer Arnold Palmer, have been described by Angel Park as the "world's most complete golf experience," and it's hard to disagree. A night-lighted driving range, a 9-hole putting course, and a golf school also form part of the complex.

A golfer playing a shot in a bunker at Angel Park Golf Club

A water feature at Wynn Golf Club

⑤ Las Vegas Paiute Golf Resort

Snow Mountain, Highway 95 (exit 95), 20 miles (32 km) N. of Las Vegas ▪ 702 658 1400

Set in the rugged desert landscape, this was the first master-planned multicourse golf resort laid out on Native American land. There are three courses in total; the Snow and Sun Mountain courses were devised by Pete Dye, who has designed many esteemed courses.

⑥ Desert Willow Golf Course

2020 W. Horizon Ridge Parkway, Henderson ▪ 702 263 4653

Entrance sign of Bali Hai Golf Club

This challenging 18-hole, 60-par course is 3,811 yards (3,485 m) long. Carved from the foothills of the Black Mountains, it is also surrounded by hazards and hilly terrain.

⑦ Las Vegas National Golf Club

MAP D4 ▪ 1911 E. Desert Inn Rd ▪ 702 734 1796

Tiger Woods played at this golf course, established in 1961, on the path to his first PGA (Professional Golf Association) victory in 1996. Soft spikes are required on this course.

⑧ Wynn Golf Club

MAP N2–3 ▪ Wynn Las Vegas, 3131 Las Vegas Blvd ▪ 702 770 4653

The luxurious Wynn is the only Las Vegas casino to boast its own golf course, located just off the Strip and landscaped to evoke the rolling hills of Georgia.

⑨ Bali Hai Golf Club

MAP C5 ▪ 5160 Las Vegas Blvd S. ▪ 702 597 2400

This course is in a prime position, just steps away from Four Seasons Hotel Las Vegas and Mandalay Bay. The South Seas-inspired design (by Brian Curley and Lee Schmidt, two well-recognized golf course architects) features 2,500 thick stands of palm trees, 7 acres (2.8 ha) of large water hazards, and about 100,000 tropical plants and flowers.

⑩ Revere Golf Club

2600 Hampton Rd, Henderson ▪ 702 259 4653

Winding through three desert canyons, this course features natural changes in elevation and spectacular views of the Las Vegas skyline. The summer rates, as at many Las Vegas courses, are lower than during other seasons.

™10 Spas and Health Clubs

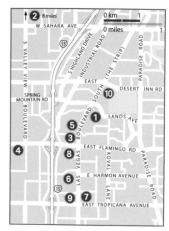

1 Canyon Ranch SpaClub

MAP P2 ■ The Venetian, 3355 Las Vegas Blvd S. ■ 702 414 3600

Residents at The Venetian can enjoy the 100-plus spa services, including skin-care treatments and 20 different styles of massage. The huge facility is also open to non-residents, as is the Canyon Ranch Café. There is a full-service salon and an expansive co-ed lounging area.

2 Spa Aquae

MAP A3 ■ J. W. Marriott Las Vegas, 221 N. Rampart Blvd ■ 702 869 7807

Treatments at this spa are not solely focused on achieving external beauty. Rather, the tailor-made spa experiences are meant to enhance health and wellness. They make use of environmentally friendly products and each experience lasts long after guests leave. Make sure you try the ayurvedic treatments.

3 Qua Baths and Spa at Caesars Palace

MAP P1–2 ■ Caesars Palace, 3570 Las Vegas Blvd S. ■ 866 782 0655

With a style that recaptures the glorious splendor that was ancient Rome, the spa incorporates Roman baths and other touches of imperial luxury. In addition to the myriad treatments on offer for both men and women, there are weight-training facilities, and several wet rooms.

4 Drift Spa

MAP B4 ■ Palms Place, 4321 Flamingo Rd W. ■ 702 944 3219

Dark stones and sleek furnishings set the scene for a chic relaxation experience at Drift Spa. The rejuvenating menu is based on the traditions of Turkey, Tunisia, Morocco, and Spain. Couples in particular will delight to find treatment rooms that feature private gardens. Other enticing features include hot and cool soaking pools, a traditional co-ed Turkish hammam, and private outdoor garden lounges.

5 The Spa at The Mirage

MAP P1–2 ■ The Mirage, 3400 Las Vegas Blvd S. ■ 702 791 7472

Feel your stresses and strains ebb away at this beautifully designed spa with its calming, neutral decor. There are several treatment rooms and an indulgent menu of treatments. There is a salon just next door, including a barbershop for men.

Calming decor of the spa at The Mirage

The sophisticated spa suite at ARIA

6 The Spa at ARIA

MAP Q1–2 ■ ARIA Resort, 3730 Las Vegas Blvd S. ■ 702 590 9600

The luxurious spa at Aria features Japanese heated-stone ganbanyoku beds, which help to purge toxins and stimulate circulation. In the Shio Salt Room guests can breathe in therapeutic salt air. In addition, there is a co-ed outdoor therapy pool on the balcony that overlooks the resort's remaining three pools and a fitness center, which offers personal training.

7 MGM Grand Spa

MAP R2 ■ MGM Grand, 3799 Las Vegas Blvd S. ■ 702 891 3077

Pamper yourself with a "Dreaming Ritual" package, which offers a foot soak, a massage, and a mud therapy treatment set to Aboriginal music. Alternatively, the excellent body exfoliation services take place in a wet room and include use of a Vichy shower, while the Morning Latte scrub is one of the signature services. You can purchase day passes for the workout room, sauna, and Jacuzzi. There's also a top hair salon overlooking the pool.

8 Spa & Salon at Bellagio

MAP Q1–2 ■ Bellagio, 3600 Las Vegas Blvd S. ■ 702 693 7472

This Italianate pampering palace combines elegant marble with cutting-edge fitness equipment. The spa's signature treatment is the Bellagio Stone Massage, which combines specially "harvested" stones prepared in a hydrobath with an energy-balancing technique to provide a thoroughly relaxing experience. Service is attentive.

9 The Spa & Salon at New York-New York

MAP R1–2 ■ New York-New York, 3790 Las Vegas Blvd S. ■ 702 740 6955

It will take far longer than a New York minute to enjoy all that is on offer at this spa. Relaxing treatments include the Intoxicating Sugar Scrub, Gel Lacquer Manicure, and the Traffic Stopper Facial. There's also a hair and beauty salon.

The lavish spa at Encore

10 The Spa at Encore

MAP N2 ■ Encore Las Vegas, 3121 Las Vegas Blvd S. ■ 702 770 3900

For a truly lavish spa experience, few places compare to the designer treatment rooms, garden villas, and couples' rooms here. The attention to detail is impeccable.

TOP 10 Shows

Trapeze act during a performance of O

1 O
MAP Q1–2 ■ Bellagio, 3600 Las Vegas Blvd S. ■ 888 488 7111 for tickets

O, staged by Cirque du Soleil, is a circus quite unlike any other. The whole show revolves around the theme of water (hence the name, as in the French *eau*). The acrobats, synchronized swimmers, divers, and characters perform in, on, and above water. Seven hydraulic lifts raise and lower the water levels throughout the performance, allowing for spectacular diving and other feats.

2 Mystère
MAP P2 ■ Treasure Island, 3300 Las Vegas Blvd S. ■ 800 392 1999 or 702 894 7722 for tickets

Created for Treasure Island, *Mystère* is an enchanting circus that – like all Cirque du Soleil productions – has a mystical thread running through it. The costumes are innovative and colorful, and together with the high-energy acrobatics, evocative dances, and vivid lighting, create an over-whelming sensory experience.

3 Penn & Teller
MAP P1 ■ Rio All-Suite Hotel and Casino, 3700 W. Flamingo Rd ■ 702 777 7776

Known as "The Bad Boys of Magic" for supposedly revealing the secrets of their tricks, Penn & Teller manage to break all of the rules of magic in this show. Edgy, provocative, and hilarious, on any given night the act can involve knives, guns, a fire-eating showgirl, or a duck. The show relies heavily on audience participation, with members invited onto the stage to take part in tricks.

4 Absinthe
MAP P1–2 ■ Caesars Palace, 3570 Las Vegas Blvd S. ■ 800 745 3000

This adults-only show is a blend of carnival and spectacle, featuring wild and outlandish acts accompanied by outrageous humor in a theater-in-the-round presentation under a big top outside Caesars. Audiences are awed by the acts performed.

5 Mac King Comedy Magic Show
MAP P2 ■ Harrah's, 3475 Las Vegas Blvd S. ■ 702 369 5222

One of the funniest and most talented magicians in Las Vegas, Mac King keeps audiences

Magician Mac King

Dancers in the mystical *Le Rêve – The Dream*

alternately spellbound and rolling in the aisles. His act includes rope tricks, a "Cloak of Invisibility," shadow puppets, and goldfish.

6 KÀ
MAP R2 ■ MGM Grand, 3799 Las Vegas Blvd S. ■ 702 531 3826 or 866 740 7711 (toll free)

This innovative theatrical spectacle from Cirque du Soleil features astonishing acrobatic performances, martial arts, puppetry, multimedia, and pyrotechnics. The colorful and entertaining show was inspired by the Egyptian belief in the *kà*, an invisible spiritual body that accompanies a person throughout their life. This theme is developed into an exciting tale about imperial twins who undertake a perilous journey into mystical lands. They face many challenges that must be overcome before they can fulfill their destiny. With impressive computer-generated effects and 80 outstanding performers, the stage is brought to life in a blaze of fire and fantasy.

7 Marriage Can Be Murder
MAP C3 ■ The D, 301 Fremont St ■ 702 388 2400

One of the last remaining Vegas dinner shows, this interactive comedy and murder mystery has the audience playing detective in solving the crime of the evening. The show takes place during the service of a three-course dinner, with actors planted in the audience, so you will be left guessing if the odd person at your table is part of the show or just a fellow guest.

8 Blue Man Group
MAP R1 ■ Luxor, 3900 Las Vegas Blvd S. ■ 800 557 7428

Unique, funny, wildly innovative, and with a contagious energy, this show is part parade and part dance party. Featuring comedy, drums, paint, and technology, it is popular with children and adults alike.

9 Le Rêve – The Dream
MAP N2 ■ Wynn Las Vegas, 3131 Las Vegas Blvd S. ■ 702 770 9966

Le Rêve depicts a colorful world inhabited by beautiful, mystifying characters. Set around a 27-ft (8-m) pool, the show features breathtaking acrobatics, provocative choreography, and artistic athleticism. Live music and elaborate effects immerse the audience in a world of fantasy, adventure, and intrigue *(see p18)*.

10 The Beatles LOVE
MAP P1–2 ■ The Mirage, 3400 Las Vegas Blvd S. ■ 702 792 7777 or 800 963 9634

Cirque du Soleil combines its magic with the exuberant spirit and timeless music of one of the best-loved bands in the world.

TOP 10 Music and Performing Arts Venues

Santana performing at The Joint

skater Katarina Witt's *Kisses on Ice* show, and a vocal performance by Andrea Bocelli.

1 The Joint

MAP Q3 ■ Hard Rock Hotel, 4455 Paradise Rd ■ 702 693 5222
■ www.thejointlasvegas.com

Since the raison d'être of the Hard Rock is to celebrate the rock-and-roll lifestyle, it's no surprise that it hosts the largest rock venue in town, capable of hosting 4,000 concertgoers in air-conditioned comfort. Veteran bands like Guns N' Roses and Journey have stayed for weeks on end *(see p43)*.

2 Mandalay Bay Events Center

MAP R2 ■ 3950 Las Vegas Blvd S. ■ 877 632 7800 ■ www. mandalaybay.com

Luciano Pavarotti inaugurated the 12,000-seat events center in 1999. Since then, performers as diverse as tenor Andrea Bocelli (with the Russian Symphony Orchestra), Justin Timberlake, and Kanye West have graced its stage. During one month in particular, the Mandalay Bay Events Center was exceptionally eclectic, staging as it did a heavy-weight bout between Evander Holyfield and John Ruiz, figure

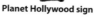

Planet Hollywood sign

3 The Smith Center for the Performing Arts

MAP K3 ■ 361 Symphony Park Ave ■ 702 749 2000
■ www.thesmithcenter.com

Featuring a 2,050-seat hall with brilliant acoustics, cabaret jazz stage, and intimate theater space, The Smith Center showcases full seasons of dance, music, and spoken word performances as well as Broadway shows. Take the time to visit Symphony Park in front of the hall and browse the artworks inside as well.

4 Pearl Theater

MAP B4 ■ Palms Casino Resort, 4321 W. Flamingo Rd ■ 702 944 3200
■ www.palms.com/pearl-theater

Just west of the Strip, this up-to-the-minute casino and concert venue is the main rival to the Hard Rock when it comes to attracting major touring rock and hip-hop artists.

5 AXIS Theater at Planet Hollywood

The 6,700-seat theater at Planet Hollywood Resort & Casino *(see p43)* features performances by Pitbull, Jennifer Lopez, and the Backstreet Boys.

6 T-Mobile Arena

MAP Q1 ■ The Park Las Vegas, 3780 Las Vegas Blvd S. ■ 702 692 1600 ■ www.t-mobilearena.com

Opened in 2016, the T-Mobile Arena boasts 20,000 seats, and hosts events such as UFC, boxing, basketball, and hockey – it is the home ground for the Vegas Golden Knights NHL hockey

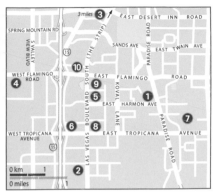

team. High-profile award shows and concerts by artists such as Jay-Z, Imagine Dragons, and Lady Gaga are also held here.

7 Thomas & Mack Center
MAP Q4 ■ University of Nevada Las Vegas, S. Maryland Parkway ■ 702 895 2787 ■ www.thomasandmack.com

Initially designed for college basketball, over the years the Thomas & Mack Center has become a site for major boxing matches as well as professional football and basketball tournaments. It has previously hosted the Vegoose Music Festival, and is one of the largest arenas in the city. In addition, the National Finals Rodeo is held here annually, drawing tens of thousands of fans. Family-style entertainment and concerts are just as popular as the sporting events.

8 David Copperfield Theater and Grand Garden Arena
MAP R2 ■ MGM Grand Hotel, 3799 Las Vegas Blvd S. ■ 800 646 7787.■ www.mgmgrand.com/entertainment

Headliners such as Tom Jones and music acts like Sting and Aerosmith regularly appear at the 740-seat David Copperfield Theater. MGM's larger 16,800-seat special-events center, the Grand Garden Arena, is used for superstar concerts,

major sporting events, and other spectaculars. It was the setting for the much-publicized Barbra Streisand Millennium Concert on New Year's Eve 1999, and has since hosted numerous high-profile concerts.

9 Paris Theater
MAP Q2 ■ Paris Las Vegas, 3655 Las Vegas Blvd S. ■ 877 374 7469

This Parisian-style theater opened in 1999 and has welcomed big names ever since, including Dennis Miller, Bobby Vinton, and Earth, Wind & Fire. It has also hosted the Broadway production of *The Producers* and is now the home of *Circus 1903*.

The auditorium of the Colosseum

10 The Colosseum
MAP P1–2 ■ Caesars Palace, 3570 Las Vegas Blvd S. ■ 866 227 5938 ■ www.thecolosseum.com

Originally built to accommodate a multi-year engagement by Celine Dion, who still appears here regularly, Caesars' astonishing 4,000-seat Colosseum, right beside the Strip, remains one of the top entertainment venues in the world. Stars such as Elton John, Rod Stewart, and Mariah Carey stage spectacular long-term residencies, while touring acts, as well as big-name comedians like Jerry Seinfeld, drop in for one-off shows.

TOP 10 Nightclubs

The Encore Beach Club pool party

① 1 OAK
MAP P1–2 ■ The Mirage Hotel & Casino, 3400 Las Vegas Blvd S. ■ 702 693 8300 ■ Open 10:30pm–4am Wed, Fri & Sat ■ www.1oaklas vegas.com ■ Admission charge

A favorite with celebrities ever since it opened with a 3-hour set from Kanye West, this 16,000-sq-ft (1,486-sq-m) venue has two rooms, a top-of-the-line sound system, and 13 oil paintings by artist Roy Nachum. The designers have a superb eye for detail, and the service is considered one of the best in Las Vegas.

② Encore Beach Club
MAP N2 ■ Wynn Las Vegas, 3131 Las Vegas Blvd S. ■ 702 770 7300 ■ Open Apr–Oct: 11am–7pm Fri & Sun, 10am–7pm Sat ■ www.encorebeachclub.com ■ Admission charge

A "dayclub" rather than a nightclub – and open, for obvious reasons, in summer only – the ultra-lavish Encore Beach Club is basically a no-expense-spared all-day pool party, given the royal seal of approval by Prince Harry in 2012.

③ TAO Nightclub
MAP P2 ■ The Venetian, 3355 Las Vegas Blvd S. ■ 702 388 8588 ■ Open 10:30pm–5am Thu–Sat; Beach Club: 11:30am–6pm daily in summer ■ www.taolasvegas.com ■ Admission charge

Originally a celeb-filled Asian bistro in New York, TAO received a Vegas makeover at The Venetian (see pp16–17) to become the fifth highest-earning nightclub in the US. Besides its restaurant and bars, the major features of this Asian-themed club are waterfalls, giant Buddha statues, and an artificial sandy beach; in summer, the pool turns into the TAO Beach club. The dance floor is small, but big-name guest DJs keep the place packed every weekend.

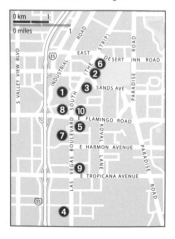

4 Light
MAP R1 ■ Mandalay Bay, 3950 Las Vegas Blvd S. ■ 702 588 5656 ■ Open 10:30pm–4am Wed, Fri & Sat ■ www.thelightvegas.com ■ Admission charge

Long the dominant force on the Las Vegas entertainment scene, Cirque du Soleil has now expanded into running nightclubs as well. World-class DJs provide the music, while Cirque performers add to the dance-floor excitement.

5 Chateau Nightclub
MAP Q2 ■ Paris Las Vegas, 3655 Las Vegas Blvd S. ■ 866 983 4279 ■ Open 10:30pm–4am Wed, Fri & Sat ■ www.chateaunights.com ■ Admission charge

Spanning more than 45,000 sq ft (4,181 sq m) and sprawled across two stories, the Chateau offers two unique nightlife experiences, including a high-energy outdoor nightclub with views of the Eiffel Tower above and the Bellagio Fountains across the street.

6 XS
MAP N2 ■ Encore Las Vegas, 3131 Las Vegas Blvd S. ■ 702 770 0097 ■ Open 10pm–4am Fri & Sat, 10:30pm–4am Sun & Mon ■ www. xslasvegas.com ■ Admission charge

Named the number one nightclub in the US by Nightclub and Bar's Top 100 for several years, this nightspot features top-of-the-line production elements, including pyrotechnics, LEDs, lasers, and an in-the-round DJ booth that can be seen from anywhere in the club.

7 MARQUEE
MAP Q1 ■ The Cosmopolitan, 3708 Las Vegas Blvd S. ■ 702 333 9000 ■ Open 10:30pm–5am Fri & Sat, 10:30pm–5am Mon, plus 11am–6pm daily in summer ■ www.marquee lasvegas.com ■ Admission charge

This massive nightclub holds seven bars and three distinct rooms – the Main Room, the Boombox, and the Library – as well as an open-air "dayclub" in summer.

8 Omnia
MAP P1–2 ■ Caesars Palace, 3570 Las Vegas Blvd S. ■ 702 785 6200 ■ Open 10pm–4am Tue & Thu–Sun ■ www.omnianightclub.com ■ Admission charge

Jaws dropped when Caesars Palace unveiled this high-tech, state-of-the-art nightclub in 2015, to replace the much-lamented Pure. As well as a constantly changing roster of big-name EDM DJs, it incorporates a vast Strip-view roof terrace.

9 Hakkasan
MAP R2 ■ MGM Grand, 3799 Las Vegas Blvd S. ■ 702 891 3838 ■ Open 10:30pm–4am Thu–Sun ■ www.hakkasanlv.com ■ Admission charge

Of course Las Vegas is home to the world's biggest nightclub, though arguably this sprawling complex is really two clubs, plus several lounges and bars. On a big night, 7,500 revelers squeeze in.

10 Drai's
MAP P2 ■ The Cromwell, 3595 Las Vegas Blvd S. ■ 702 777 3800 ■ Open 10pm–4am Thu–Sat; Drai's Beach Club: 11am–6pm Fri–Sun in summer ■ www.draislv.com ■ Admission charge

This colossal club, open both day and night during the summer, enjoys fabulous views of the Strip from its prime position on the Cromwell's specially strengthened roof, and features live performers as well as DJs.

Outdoor rooftop pools at Drai's

TOP 10 Bars and Lounges on the Strip

Parasol Up, Parasol Down

1 Parasol Up, Parasol Down

MAP N2 ▪ Wynn Las Vegas, 3131 Las Vegas Blvd S. ▪ Open 11–3am Sun–Thu, 11–4am Fri & Sat

This matching pair of colorful, classy cocktail bars, set one above the other on the central stairwell of Wynn Las Vegas *(see pp18–19)*, are playfully decorated with bright umbrellas. They give a great vantage point for the nightly light and music show on the Lake of Dreams.

2 Ghostbar

MAP B4 ▪ The Palms, 4321 Flamingo Rd W. ▪ 702 942 6832 ▪ Open 10pm–4am daily ▪ www. palms.com ▪ Admission charge

One of the most futuristic and stylish lounges in the city, the Palms' *(see p38)* Ghostbar is best known for its

"ghost deck," which, at 55 floors high, offers unforgettable views. Attracts a young crowd.

3 Peppermill Fireside Lounge

MAP N3 ▪ 2985 Las Vegas Blvd S. ▪ 702 735 4177 ▪ Open 24 hours ▪ www.peppermilllasvegas.com

This much-loved veteran bar is one of the few survivors of the Las Vegas that existed before the corporations moved in. However, with its pink neon, banquette seating, and flame-spouting fire pit, it's every bit as over-the-top as the casino lounges.

4 Nine Fine Irishmen

MAP R2 ▪ New York–New York, 3790 Las Vegas Blvd S. ▪ 702 740 6463 ▪ Open 11am–11pm Mon–Fri, 9am–11pm Sat & Sun ▪ www.newyorknewyork.com/en/restaurants/nine-fine-irishmen ▪ Admission charge

If this casino bar in New York–New York *(see p42)* looks just like a real Irish pub, that's because it is – they shipped the whole thing over from Ireland. There is nightly Irish entertainment, too.

5 Cleopatra's Barge

MAP P1–2 ▪ Caesars Palace, 3570 Las Vegas Blvd S. ▪ 702 731 7333 ▪ Open 7pm–3am Tue–Sat

Amazingly enough, this lounge bar really is located on a floating barge,

The sleek interior of Ghostbar, on the 55th floor of the Palms

moored in little more than a puddle in the heart of Caesars Palace (see p42). Despite its ancient Egyptian appearance, however, it only dates back to the 1960s.

6 Minus5° Ice Bar
MAP R1 ■ Mandalay Bay, 3930 Las Vegas Blvd S. ■ 702 740 5800 ■ Open 11–2am Sun–Thu, 11–3am Fri & Sat ■ www.minus5 experience.com ■ Admission charge

Everything in this place really is made out of ice – the glasses, the seating, and yes, even the bar itself. Naturally you're provided with warm clothing to help you grin and bear it.

Decor made of ice at Minus5° Ice Bar

7 The Dorsey
MAP P2 ■ The Venetian, 3355 Las Vegas Blvd S. ■ 702 414 1945 ■ Open 3pm–4am daily

True cocktail culture is celebrated at The Dorsey, along with old school service standards. The handcrafted cocktail menu was designed by award-winning bartender Sam Ross, of NYC's Attaboy fame. In the evenings, renowned DJs spin both classics and newer tunes that fit the relaxed vibe.

8 Gilley's Saloon
MAP P2 ■ TI, 3300 Las Vegas Blvd S. ■ 702 894 7111 ■ Open 11–2am Sun–Thu, 11–4am Fri & Sat ■ www.gilleyslasvegas.com ■ Admission charge for live music

There is always a party atmosphere in this lively, down-to-earth bar where you can ride a mechanical rodeo bull, take a lesson in line dancing, or catch one of the live bands that frequently play country music here.

9 Beerhaus
MAP Q1 ■ The Park Las Vegas 3784 Las Vegas Blvd S. ■ 702 692 2337 ■ Open 11–1am Mon–Thu & Sun, 11–2am Fri, 10–2am Sat

Located within The Park, this beer-centric pub offers more than 60 craft beers with an emphasis on local brews. There are plenty of games such as jenga, connect four, ping pong, shuffleboard, and foosball. Expect a packed house when live bands play from Thursday to Sunday.

10 Chandelier
MAP Q2 ■ The Cosmopolitan, 3708 Las Vegas Blvd S. ■ Open 24 hours

A vast, shimmering chandelier hangs down through three floors of the Cosmopolitan casino (see p39), and it is circled at all three levels by this chic bar. There is a cool, relaxed lounge on the uppermost level, while the central level is a full-fledged nightclub.

The Cosmopolitan's Chandelier

🔟 Gourmet Restaurants

1 Le Cirque
MAP Q1–2 ■ **Bellagio, 3600 Las Vegas Blvd S.** ■ **702 693 8865** ■ **$$$**

Renowned for its sumptuous French cuisine, this opulent and much-lauded restaurant, an offshoot of the Manhattan original, is set in a prime position by the Bellagio's lake (see pp14–15). The six-course tasting menu, available with wine pairings, abounds in caviar and truffles.

Picasso restaurant

2 Picasso
MAP Q1–2 ■ **Bellagio, 3600 Las Vegas Blvd S.** ■ **702 693 7223** ■ **$$$**

The room is exquisite, with original Picasso paintings adorning the walls and a carpet designed by Pablo Picasso's son, Claude, underfoot. The Spanish-born chef, Julian Serrano, creates contemporary French dishes with an Iberian accent. Among the delights on offer are Maine lobster salad, pan-seared scallop, sautéed steak of foie gras, and sautéed fillet of halibut.

3 Julian Serrano
MAP Q1 ■ **ARIA Resort, 3730 Las Vegas Blvd S.** ■ **877 230 2742** ■ **$$$**

This stylish, contemporary restaurant, adjoining the main lobby of the ARIA Resort (see p24), serves its namesake chef's take on Spanish tapas, with delectable interpretations of his native fare. Larger plates are available as well, including paella.

4 L'Atelier de Joël Robuchon
MAP R2 ■ **MGM Grand, 3799 Las Vegas Blvd S.** ■ **702 891 7925** ■ **$$$**

A feast for both the palate and the eyes, the food at this outstanding restaurant is predominantly French, with Asian and Spanish influences. Signature dishes include L'Artichaut, a semisoft boiled egg on a carbonara of pearl pasta with smoked bacon and baby artichoke.

5 Twist by Pierre Gagnaire
MAP Q2 ■ **Mandarin Oriental, 3752 Las Vegas Blvd S.** ■ **702 590 3172** ■ **$$$**

Pierre Gagnaire, who is among the most inventive of the new generation of French chefs, "twists" classic dishes to create everything from sea-urchin mousse to foie gras ice cream. This is his only US outlet, set within the 5-star Mandarin Oriental hotel in CityCenter (see p25).

The sleek interior of Nobu

complemented by dishes such as seared Hudson Valley foie gras with spiced pineapple bread pudding and bourbon reduction.

8 Bouchon
MAP P2 ■ The Venetian, 3355 Las Vegas Blvd ■ 702 414 6200 ■ $$$

Established by one of the most renowned chefs in America, Thomas Keller, this eatery serves up traditional French-bistro fare with style. The food is cooked using only top-quality ingredients, and the unique wine list on offer ensures the perfect accompaniment to each dish.

6 Nobu
MAP P1 ■ Caesars Palace, 3570 Las Vegas Blvd S. ■ 702 785 6628 ■ $$$

Diners all over the world simply cannot seem to resist the exquisite fusion cuisine of the Japanese-Peruvian chef Nobu Matsuhisa. Signature dishes include black cod miso, rock shrimp tempura and yellowtail Sashimi.

9 Estiatorio Milos
MAP Q2 ■ The Cosmopolitan, 3708 Las Vegas Blvd S. ■ 702 698 7930 ■ $$$

This gorgeous Greek restaurant, decorated in true Classic style, specializes in delicately prepared fish, which are flown in specially each day from Athens. The lunch menu guarantees great value.

7 Charlie Palmer Steak
MAP R1 ■ Four Seasons Hotel, 3960 Las Vegas Blvd S. ■ 702 632 5000 ■ $$$

American celebrity chef Charlie Palmer's steakhouse offers a menu featuring traditional cuts including filet mignon and bone-in rib eye,

10 Scarpetta
MAP Q2 ■ The Cosmopolitan, 3708 Las Vegas Blvd S. ■ 877 893 2003 ■ $$$

Appropriately enough, the finest Italian restaurant in Las Vegas enjoys views of the Bellagio fountains. Chef Scott Conant, who draws his influences from Japan as well as Europe, insists on describing the menu as "new Italian."

Italian restaurant Scarpetta

For a key to restaurant price ranges see p86

⭑10 Vegas Dining Experiences

Open-air dining at Mon Ami Gabi

what America's really having for dinner, why not drop in at one of the very few stand-alone options on the Strip? This classic, gleaming, all-night burger joint is located directly across from the CityCenter complex.

1 Mon Ami Gabi
MAP Q2 ■ 3655 Las Vegas Blvd S. ■ 702 944 4224 ■ www.mon amigabi.com ■ $$

The first, and still the best, Las Vegas restaurant where you can eat in the open air, this Parisian-style brasserie right next to the Strip offers beautifully authentic French classics, from onion soup to steak frites.

2 Burger Bar
MAP R2 ■ Mandalay Place, 3930 Las Vegas Blvd S. ■ 702 632 9363 ■ www.burger-bar.com ■ $$

So-called "gourmet burgers" are all the rage these days, but French chef Hubert Keller got there ahead of the rest. Here, fancy cocktails and milkshakes are served along with "the ultimate burger experience." Meats on offer include turkey, lamb, and buffalo as well as top-quality Wagyu beef.

3 Fatburger
MAP Q2 ■ 3763 Las Vegas Blvd S. ■ 702 736 4733 ■ www.fat burger.com ■ $

If you are getting tired of casino restaurants, and fancy a taste of

4 Eiffel Tower Restaurant
MAP Q2 ■ Paris, 3655 Las Vegas Blvd S. ■ 702 948 6937 ■ www. eiffeltowerrestaurant.com ■ $$$

Where else can you dine in style inside the Eiffel Tower, while taking in the wonderful views over a legendary city? Well, in Paris, France, of course – but that doesn't have the spectacle of the Bellagio fountains opposite.

5 Triple George Grill
MAP J4 ■ 201 N. Third St ■ 702 384 2761 ■ www.triplegeorge grill.com ■ $$$

This Downtown steakhouse, with the feel of an old-time speakeasy, is regularly packed with local lawyers and politicians. The eponymous George, incidentally, is a Las Vegas slang term for a big tipper, and all-round decent guy (as opposed to a "stiff," who never tips, no matter how much they win).

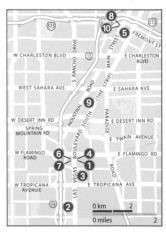

For a key to restaurant price ranges see p86

Interior of Jean Philippe Patisserie

American cuisine, courtesy of Boston chef Todd English, as you watch the famous fountains at play.

⑧ Oscar's • Beef • Booze • Broads
MAP J4 ▪ The Plaza, 1 Main St ▪ 702 386 7227 ▪ www.oscarslv.com ▪ $$$
This old-fashioned Downtown steakhouse, housed in the strange glass dome of the Plaza *(see p93)* with views over Fremont Street, is a real only-in-Vegas experience. The eponymous Oscar is the owner and the former mayor of the city – the current mayor is his wife – while the "broads" are the hostesses, who will tell you the history of Las Vegas while you dine.

⑨ Top of the World
MAP M3 ▪ Stratosphere Casino, Hotel & Tower, 2000 Las Vegas Blvd S. ▪ 702 380 7711 ▪ www.topoftheworldlv.com ▪ $$$
Perched at a height of 844 ft (257 m) on the top floor of the Stratosphere, a short distance from the north end of the Strip, this entire dining room rotates every 80 minutes. It is regularly hailed as the most romantic restaurant for dinner in the city, but if you really want to enjoy the views, come at lunchtime.

⑥ Jean Philippe Patisserie
MAP Q1–2 ▪ Bellagio, 3600 Las Vegas Blvd S. ▪ 702 590 7227 ▪ www.jpchocolates.com ▪ $
For sheer, mouthwatering spectacle, Las Vegas holds nothing to match the amazing chocolate fountain at this Bellagio bakery. Cascading in enticing coils from floor to ceiling around the entire room, it is the largest one in the world, and lures in customers for crêpes, pastries, and coffee as well as to appreciate the chocolate fountain itself.

⑩ Hash House A Go Go
MAP J4 ▪ The Plaza, 1 Main St ▪ 702 386 4646 ▪ www.hashhouse agogo.com ▪ $$
There are five Hash House A Go Go outlets in Las Vegas, but its all-American diner aesthetic and its menu of "twisted farm food" (healthy country-style classics served in oversize portions) make it an especially good fit with Downtown.

⑦ Todd English's Olives
MAP Q1–2 ▪ 3600 Las Vegas Blvd S. ▪ 702 693 8865 ▪ www.bellagio.com ▪ $$
There are several restaurants at Bellagio that offer the option of alfresco dining, but this is the nicest of the lot. Enjoy the zestful, Italian-influenced, contemporary

Hash House A Go Go's distinctive sign

🔟 Buffets

1 Le Village Buffet
MAP Q2 ■ Paris Las Vegas, 3655 Las Vegas Blvd S. ■ 702 946 7000 ■ $$

An innovative blend of offerings at the Paris Las Vegas, including omelets, imported cheeses, bouillabaisse, wild mushroom bisque, lamb, venison, prime rib steak, and huge shrimp, all followed by a wealth of indulgent French-inspired desserts.

2 Wicked Spoon
MAP Q2 ■ The Cosmopolitan, 3708 Las Vegas Blvd S. ■ 702 698 7000 ■ $$

Tucked away at the back of The Cosmopolitan's upper level, this bright buffet has quickly established itself as a favorite with lunching locals. Unusually, most dishes are displayed as individual servings, but you can help yourself to however many you want. Brunch here is equally popular.

3 Bacchanal Buffet
MAP P1 ■ Caesars Palace, 3570 Las Vegas Blvd ■ 702 731 7928 ■ $$$

This show-stopping buffet at Caesars Palace offers more than 500 fresh dishes and about 15 chef's specials daily. With its chic, upscale interiors and contemporary food presentation,

the Bacchanal Buffet is worth a visit for its enormous variety of food. Choose from the air, wood, and water-themed sections of the dining rooms. Don't forget to try the fried chicken and waffles, as well as the red velvet pancakes.

4 Bellagio Buffet
MAP Q1–2 ■ Bellagio, 3600 Las Vegas Blvd S. ■ 888 987 6667 ■ $$

A large, sumptuous dining buffet offering more than 60 dishes, ranging from Japanese and Chinese to Italian and new American cuisine. Specialties include all the shrimps you can eat, wild duck breast, and roast venison. Save room for the decadent cheesecake.

The upscale Bacchanal Buffet at Caesars Palace

Elegant Wynn Buffet

5 Wynn Buffet
MAP N2 ■ Wynn Las Vegas, 3131 Las Vegas Blvd S. ■ 702 770 7000 ■ $$

A very strong contender for the best buffet in town, this no-expense-spared extravaganza has the feel of a gourmet restaurant, with individual dishes labeled in appetizing detail. The selection is superb: 15 live cooking stations prepare seafood and roast meats. Save room for the sweetshop station and gelato bar.

6 Flavors Buffet
MAP P2 ■ Harrah's, 3475 Las Vegas Blvd S. ■ 702 693 6060 ■ $

The Caesars group of hotels has a reputation for excellent food. Although the buffet offerings at the Flavors Buffet are not as unusual as those of some competitors, the standards of preparation and service are consistently high. Customers in the know go for the salads and extremely attractive desserts.

7 The Buffet at ARIA
MAP Q1 ■ ARIA, 3730 Las Vegas Blvd S. ■ 702 590 7111 ■ $$

Aria's bright, stylish dining room doesn't offer quite as many dishes as most, but that's because the chefs concentrate on creating one or two excellent items for each cuisine. The Indian meats and breads, baked in a tandoori oven, are wonderful.

8 Studio B Buffet
MAP P4 ■ The M Resort, 12300 Las Vegas Blvd S., Henderson ■ 702 797 1000 ■ $

Integrating a top-notch restaurant with live-action cooking, this buffet is unlike any other in Las Vegas. The 600-seat restaurant serves some of the best patisserie desserts, including the popular mini crème brûlée, and numerous chocolate souffles, cookies, and tarts.

9 Golden Nugget Buffet
MAP K4 ■ Golden Nugget Hotel, 129 Fremont St ■ 702 385 7111 ■ $

There are around 60 buffet rooms in Las Vegas, and most could not be described as aesthetically lovely. The setting of the Golden Nugget, however, is just that. The dishes are pretty tasty, too: don't miss the fresh carved turkey and old-fashioned bread pudding.

The Buffet at ARIA

10 Carnival World & Seafood Buffet
MAP P1 ■ Rio All-Suite Hotel & Casino, 3700 W. Flamingo Rd ■ 888 396 2483 ■ $$$

The successful Village Seafood Buffet merged with the Carnival World Buffet in November 2015 and continues to be a favorite with local residents. With over 300 options, fresh crab, shrimp, oysters, and other seafood are flown in daily.

For a key to restaurant price ranges see p86

⓾ Places to Shop

The boutique-lined Via Bellagio

① Via Bellagio
MAP Q1–2 ■ Bellagio, 3600 Las Vegas Blvd S.

Simply walking along Via Bellagio *(see also p14)* is an unforgettable experience. The boutiques are so opulent as to be intimidating: even if you dare not step inside, then at least the entrances to Fendi, Chanel, Gucci, and others are large enough to see inside. Tiffany's windows are especially dazzling during the holiday season.

② Fashion Show Mall
MAP N2 ■ 3200 Las Vegas Blvd S.

This upscale shoppers' paradise boasts Saks Fifth Avenue and Nordstrom department stores. The mall also hosts regular fashion shows and events.

Crystals at CityCenter

③ Miracle Mile Shops
MAP Q2 ■ Within Planet Hollywood Resort and Casino, 3667 Las Vegas Blvd S.

British fashion at French Connection, leisure wear at Urban Outfitters, and beautiful accessories at Swarovski are located here. There are over 200 specialty shops and restaurants, including Club Tattoo, featuring top tattoo artists.

④ The Forum Shops at Caesars Palace

These shops are laid out along pseudo-Roman streets within the Caesars Palace resort complex, characterized by two-story storefronts topped with statues of Roman senators. Along with wares from Europe, American design is featured at stores such as Abercrombie & Fitch, Coach, and Brooks Brothers. During the holiday season, The Forum Shops are particularly popular. An expansion added a further 175,000 sq ft (16,258 sq m) and additional levels to the complex *(see also pp20–21)*.

⑤ Crystals at CityCenter
MAP Q1–2 ■ 3720 Las Vegas Blvd S.

Featuring the highest concentration of designer flagship stores in the world, this high-end shopping area lures visitors with retailers including Prada, Gucci, Versace, Hermes, Valentino, Ermenegildo, Sisley, Jimmy Choo, Tiffany & Co., and Dolce & Gabbana.

6 The Galleria at Sunset
MAP E5 ▪ 1300 W. Sunset Rd, Henderson

One of the city's residential malls, the Galleria at Sunset offers department store shopping and down-to-earth services, such as jewelry repair, free jewelry cleaning, alterations and tailoring, hairstyling, beauty treatments, and gift wrapping.

7 The Shoppes at Mandalay Place
MAP R1–2 ▪ Mandalay Bay, 3950 Las Vegas Blvd S.

An eclectic selection of shops located on a 100,000-sq-ft (9,290-sq-m) sky bridge, Mandalay Place connects The Shoppes at Mandalay Bay with Luxor Hotel and Casino. Stores include The Art of Music, which sells autographed memorabilia. There are plenty of restaurants and eateries as well, including Minus5°, one of Las Vegas's ice bars (see p65).

8 Town Square Las Vegas
MAP C5 ▪ 6605 Las Vegas Blvd S.

Take some time out from the Strip's sensory overload at this large outdoor shopping center with its village-like storefronts and quaint streetscapes. The 120-plus stores include big-name favorites such as Abercrombie & Fitch, H&M, and Apple. There is plenty of entertainment with an 18-screen movie theater and a kids' playground, boasting a 42-ft- (13-m-) tall treehouse and 30 pop-jet fountains, along with a GameWorks Entertainment Center that has LAN gaming facilities.

9 The Grand Canal Shoppes at The Venetian
MAP P2 ▪ The Venetian, 3355 Las Vegas Blvd S.

Located on the second floor of The Venetian (see pp16–17), the emphasis at Grand Canal Shoppes is on European elegance. Exquisite goods for sale include handmade Venetian lace, glass, and masks as well as silks, shoes, and jewelry from various European countries.

The Grand Canal Shoppes

Part of the pleasure of shopping at this mall is the distinctive ambience – it may not be quite like the real Venice, but the experience is enjoyable nonetheless.

10 Las Vegas North Premium Outlets
MAP K3 ▪ 875 S. Grand Central Parkway

This colossal mall features separate outlets run by big-name designer brands, such as Adidas and Lacoste, which sell discontinued product lines and factory-line rejects for highly reduced prices. The owners run another mall of the same name on Las Vegas Boulevard south of the Strip, but this one offers more discounts.

TOP 10 Las Vegas for Free

Pete Vallee performing as Big Elvis

1 Big Elvis
MAP P2 ■ The Piano Bar, Harrah's, 3475 Las Vegas Blvd S. ■ 702 369 5111 ■ Open 2–6pm Mon, Wed & Fri ■ www.caesars.com/harrahs-las-vegas/shows/big-elvis

If you are here to see Elvis, then you have come to the right place – the large and highly likable impersonator Pete Vallee puts on a fabulous free show on weekday afternoons, performing the greatest hits of "the king of rock and roll."

2 Fremont Street Experience

Not only have they put a roof over Downtown Las Vegas, but after dark it becomes a vast screen, onto which is projected extravagant nightly light-and-sound shows. Bands also play on street-level stages, and there is no shortage of street performers to add to the entertainment (see p91).

3 Wildlife Habitat
Stroll into the tropical gardens of the Flamingo Las Vegas and discover the unexpected treat of a lagoon that is home to a flock of genuine (and extremely pink) Chilean flamingoes. Pelicans, ibis and tiny hummingbirds can also be seen lurking amid the foliage (see p53).

4 Circus Entertainment
Deep in the heart of Circus Circus, a parade of jugglers, acrobats, clowns, and even stunt bikers lives up to the original theme of the casino when it was first opened in the 1960s. There are free performances every half hour between 11am and midnight (see p81).

5 The Mirage Volcano
Crowds of onlookers still gather on the sidewalk of the Strip to admire the nightly pyro-technics of the famous volcano outside the Mirage (see p83), which first erupted back in 1989, and now features a thunderous sound-track by the drummer from the 1960s rock band the Grateful Dead.

6 The Las Vegas Sign
MAP C5 ■ 5100 Las Vegas Blvd S. ■ Open 24 hours daily

First unveiled in 1959, this iconic neon sign, situated half a mile (1 km) south of Mandalay Bay Events Center (see p60), has been listed on the National Register of Historic Places since 2009. Only drivers heading south along the Strip can access it; bring your selfie stick along and get a souvenir photo with it.

The iconic Las Vegas sign

7 Fountains of Bellagio
Spouting high, spurting far, swirling sinuously, and swaying seductively, the spectacular displays of the Bellagio fountains, submerged in the waters of its placid Strip-front lake, are the best-loved free show in all of Las Vegas (see p81).

8 Million-Dollar Photo
MAP J4 ■ Binions, 128 E. Fremont St ■ 702 382 1600 ■ Open 9am–11:30pm daily ■ www.binions.com

Visitors to Binions casino in Downtown Las Vegas can pose for souvenir photos with a million dollars in cash. The only catch is that you have to wait half an hour before the print of your photo is ready to be picked up.

9 Fall of Atlantis
MAP P1 ■ Forum Shops, 3500 Las Vegas Blvd S. ■ 702 893 3807 ■ Performances 11am–10pm daily (to 11pm Fri & Sat) ■ www.forum shops.com

With their artificial sky and ancient Roman decor, the Forum Shops make a great free show in their own right, but you can't beat the moment when the animatronic "statues" in its Atlantis fountain spring to life.

10 M&M's World
MAP R2 ■ 3785 Las Vegas Blvd S. ■ 702 740 2504 ■ Open 9am–midnight daily ■ www.mmsworld.com

Granted, kids are more likely than adults to thrill at the prospect of this "retail-entertainment attraction" spread over four stories, but surprisingly enough, they're not wrong. It's actually great fun, and includes a free 3-D movie starring the M&M characters Red and Yellow.

Entrance to M&M's World

TOP 10 MONEY-SAVING TIPS

Gamblers are served free drinks

1 As long as you are gambling, the casino will ply you with free alcoholic drinks – but be sure to tip.

2 For better hotel rates, visit on weekdays – and avoid conventions, holidays, and other important events.

3 Use Caesars' 24-hour "Buffet of Buffets" to dine at 8pm one night and 7pm the next. You will also save money by eating your big meal of the day at lunchtime, when buffets usually cost a few dollars less than at night.

4 Discount tickets for shows are sold online, and at 10 kiosks on the Strip and Fremont Street, by Tix4Tonight. www.tix4tonight.com

5 Register with the "players' clubs" in casinos in order to benefit from assorted discounts.

6 Only rent a car when you actually need it – and when you do, you will get better rates at the airport than from your hotel.

7 Ask about discount coupons in your hotel, and look for more in the free magazines you can pick up from the information center run by the Las Vegas Convention & Visitors Authority. www.lvcva.com

8 Use the city buses, and buy an $8 24-hour pass or a $20 3-day pass. www.catride.com

9 Many shows offer two-for-one deals on tickets; ask at the ticket counters.

10 To save money on entertainment, check out the calendar sections of local papers and magazines, where free events are often listed. Almost every casino lounge puts on free live music to entice people in.

TOP 10 Festivals and Annual Events

Chinese New Year decorations

1 Chinese New Year
MAP B4 ■ Chinatown Plaza, Spring Mountain Rd ■ Late Jan–mid-Feb

Chinese New Year festivities center on Chinatown Plaza (see p97). Highlights include the traditional Chinese lion dance, firecrackers, Chinese food, and feng shui as it pertains to the New Year.

2 St. Patrick's Day Celebration
MAP K4 ■ Mar 17 or closest weekend

St. Patrick's parties are held at various restaurants and bars, with the main celebration at the Fremont Street Experience (see p91). Crowd-pleasers include a full line-up of music, entertainment, green beer (with green food coloring), and traditional Irish dishes.

3 Cinco de Mayo
All around the city ■ May 5 or closest weekend

The Mexican national holiday, commemorating the victory of the Mexicans over the French in 1862, is celebrated up and down the Strip and around Las Vegas. Traditional Hispanic music is played in performance spaces, margaritas are poured freely, and typical food like tacos and tamales are served at celebration spots around the city.

4 Electric Daisy Carnival
Las Vegas Motor Speedway, 7000 Las Vegas Blvd N. ■ May ■ lasvegas.electricdaisycarnival.com

This three-day electronic dance music festival features art, carnival rides, circus-style performances, and electronic dance music DJs. It has been known to attract more than 30,000 revelers each year.

5 Greek Food Festival
MAP B5 ■ St. John the Baptist Greek Orthodox Church, 5300 S. El Camino Las Vegas ■ 702 221 8245 ■ Sep or Oct ■ www.lasvegas greekfestival.com

Ever since the early 1970s, the Las Vegas Greek Food Festival has celebrated all the aromas, sounds, tastes, and traditions of Greece. The festival runs for four days and includes continuous dancing with live Greek bands; fabulous Greek food; and stalls with gifts, jewelry, and art.

6 Pacific Islands Festival
MAP G6 ■ Henderson Events Plaza, 200 S. Water St ■ 702 267 2171 ■ Sep

The many Pacific Rim peoples who live in the Las Vegas area celebrate their various heritages with traditional entertainment, cultural exhibits, and fashion boutiques. Food includes everything from *kimchi* and *poi* to potstickers and teriyaki.

7 Halloween Haunted Houses
Late Oct

Several companies have set up dozens of haunted houses in parking lots, community centers, and parks. Some are heavy on the scare factor while others are more like fun houses, with warped mirrors and a few twisted surprises.

⑧ National Finals Parties
Various venues ■ Dec

During the National Finals Rodeo, all of Las Vegas seems to go country – wearing jeans and boots. Casinos bring in country music bands, and line dancing is encouraged. The free entertainment magazines are the best sources of information about what's going on where. The Cowboy Christmas Gift Show is one of the most popular events.

⑨ New Year's Eve
Dec 31

Nowhere celebrates New Year's Eve quite like Las Vegas. The entire city goes into party mode, with big-name headliners performing in the major theaters, and special events in all the nightclubs. Hotel rates, too, are at their highest. At midnight, the Strip's skyline fills with firework displays.

New Year's Eve fireworks

⑩ Magical Forest
MAP B3 ■ Opportunity Village, 6300 W. Oakey Blvd ■ 702 259 3741 ■ Nov–Jan

Opportunity Village, an organization that helps the mentally disabled, raises funds by creating a Magical Forest with hundreds of decorated Christmas trees, holiday lights, and a gingerbread house display. Nightly entertainment appropriate for all ages, and a fun passenger train make this a good family choice.

TOP 10 SPORTING EVENTS

National Finals Rodeo

1 National Finals Rodeo
Thomas & Mack Center ■ early Dec
Cowboys compete for million-dollar prizes at the USA's premier rodeo.

2 World Championship Boxing
Caesars Palace, MGM Grand, Mandalay Bay, T-Mobile Arena, Thomas & Mack Center
Las Vegas is still the premier city for big-name title bouts.

3 NASCAR Cup Series
Las Vegas Motor Speedway ■ Mar
Watch Sprint Cup car practices and races.

4 Baseball
Cashman Field, 850 Las Vegas Blvd N. ■ Apr–Labor Day
Watch the Las Vegas 51s on their home ground.

5 UNLV Sports Events
Thomas & Mack Center, Sam Boyd Stadium, UNLV campus ■ Sep–May
The university's Rebels basketball, football, and baseball teams are hometown favorites.

6 NHRA Summit Nationals
Las Vegas Motor Speedway, 7000 Las Vegas Blvd N. ■ Dates vary
Dragsters battle for supremacy.

7 World Series of Poker
Rio All-Suites Hotel & Casino ■ May–Jul
Poker players compete for millions.

8 PBR Championship
Thomas & Mack Center ■ Oct or Nov
Professional bull-riding competition.

9 Las Vegas Triathlon
Lake Mead ■ Sep
Sprint, Olympic, and half races.

10 Shriners Hospitals for Children Open
TPC Summerlin ■ Oct
Attracts PGA golfers for a good cause.

Las Vegas
Area by Area

View across the Fountains of Bellagio to
the replica Eiffel Tower at Paris Las Vegas

顶10 The Strip

Walk along the Strip and you'll see that some of the best things in Las Vegas life are free – especially when it comes to sightseeing and entertainment. It costs nothing to walk through the hotel-casinos, and you can window-shop to your heart's content in their shopping promenades. The hotels' architecture makes for an attraction in its own right: where else would you find an Egyptian sphinx, the Eiffel Tower, Venetian canals, and a medieval castle on the same street? In addition, some hotel-casinos have free entertainment going on outside their doors.

Flamingo Wildlife Habitat

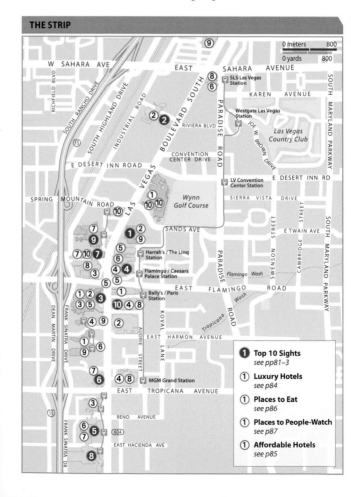

THE STRIP

Top 10 Sights
see pp81–3

Luxury Hotels
see p84

Places to Eat
see p86

Places to People-Watch
see p87

Affordable Hotels
see p85

Gondolas at The Venetian

1 The Venetian

Sheldon Adelson, the owner of the largest hotel-casino on the Strip, enjoyed his honeymoon in Venice, Italy, so much that he brought the entire city home with him. At least, that's how it looks – as well as its showpiece Grand Canal, complete with singing gondoliers, The Venetian includes replicas of landmarks, such as the Rialto Bridge, St. Mark's Square, and the Doge's Palace. Simply stroll in off the Strip and you can admire its art and architecture for free; its 7,000-plus hotel rooms, and its restaurants, nightclubs, and shops, cost a little more, of course (see pp16–17).

2 Circus Circus
Performances every half hour, 11am–midnight

Over the course of more than 40 years, Circus Circus has entertained hundreds of thousands of spectators with its impressive shows. Stars have included the Flying Farfans of Argentina and the miniature-bicycle rider Charles Charles of Paris. With performances taking place every half hour, you can pop back for different shows and catch a wide variety of acts (see p85).

3 Fountains of Bellagio
Performances every half hour, 3–8pm Mon–Fri, noon–8pm Sat, 11am–7pm Sun. Every 15 mins 8pm–midnight Mon–Sat, 7pm–midnight Sun

More than 1,000 fountains perform a water ballet above Lake Bellagio, in defiance of the parched, baking desert that surrounds the city.

Soaring as high as 240 ft (73 m) in the air, the cascading water is choreographed to classical music. Bellagio and the other properties in the MGM Mirage group use incandescent lighting rather than neon, which makes the lit-up Italian village surrounding the lake a lovely backdrop for the dancing waters (see p84).

4 Flamingo Wildlife Habitat
Open 24 hours

The 15-acre (6-ha) habitat at Flamingo Las Vegas, improbably located in the heart of the Las Vegas Strip, is home to 70 birds, including Chilean flamingoes, pelicans, and black swans, more than 300 fish, and 30 turtles. It is a welcome oasis in the often overwhelming desert environment (see p85).

5 Luxor

A strikingly modern twist on an ancient classic, the unique 30-floor, black-glass pyramid of the Luxor is one of the most recognizable landmarks in Las Vegas. The structure is topped with a 42.3-billion candela (315,000-watt) light beam, a Vegas icon, which is visible from space and is the strongest beam of light in the world. The hotel-casino's awe-inspiring atrium, at 29 million cubic ft (820,000 cubic m), is one of the largest in the world. A 10-story sphinx (larger than the Egyptian original) guards the premises. Luxor is also home to the Cirque du Soleil production *Criss Angel Mindfreak Live!*, and *Bodies... The Exhibition* (see p42).

Luxor's pyramid and sphinx

The New York-New York hotel-casino complex

6 New York-New York

More manageable in scale than most of the Strip giants, while still featuring facsimiles of everything from the Brooklyn Bridge to the Empire State Building, this endearing microcosm of Manhattan is irresistible, both inside and out. Most of its replica buildings are approximately half life-size; amazingly, though, the Statue of Liberty stands twice as high as the original. Thrill-seekers can circle the whole lot in the tiny yellow cabs of the Big Apple Coaster (see p43).

7 The Forum Shops at Caesars Palace

Use the first freestanding escalator of its kind in the United States to reach the shopping destinations of your choice, or ride it just for fun. In the Roman Great Hall, check out the 50,000-gallon (189,304-liter) saltwater aquarium, home to hundreds of colorful tropical fish. Keep an eye out for the spectacle of divers feeding the fish, which happens twice a day, usually in the afternoon. Some of the shops provide entertainment, but often the most fun can be had by taking a break on a bench to watch the shoppers from around the world (see pp20–21).

8 Shark Reef Aquarium at Mandalay Bay

Open 10am–8pm Sun–Thu, 10am–10pm Fri & Sat (10am–10pm daily in summer) ■ **Admission charge**

It is truly awe-inspiring to wander within the special walkways of the 1.3-million-gallon (4.9-million-liter) aquarium and observe the thousands of wonderful sea creatures swimming together. Look out for the arowana dragon fish – and, of course, 11 different species of shark (see p84).

AN EXPANDING CITY

In the past, Las Vegas saw very rapid expansion, with the constant construction of hotels, condominiums, and shopping facilities. In the mid-2000s, the city hit a sharp economic decline and many projects were put on hold or abandoned altogether. Today, Las Vegas is starting to grow again, but this time growth is both cautious and calculated.

9 The Mirage Volcano

Erupts 8pm & 9pm Sun–Thu, 8pm, 9pm & 10pm Fri & Sat ■ www.mirage.com/en/amenities/volcano.html

With displays like this, it is hardly surprising that the Mirage, when it was opened in 1989, is said to have triggered the 1990s hotel-building boom. The man-made, multimillion-dollar volcano spews fire 100 ft (30 m) into the air every night. Ingenious lighting and steam effects convey the drama of lava flows, while loudspeakers broadcast vivid sound effects featuring the work of Grateful Dead drummer Mickey Hart (see p84).

The Mirage Volcano

10 Paris Las Vegas

The iconic Eiffel Tower and Arc de Triomphe are faithfully and impressively reproduced at Paris Las Vegas, albeit on a smaller scale than the originals. You can buy fresh baguettes from a "street vendor," and nibble it to the strains of tunes by the great Maurice Chevalier, as interpreted by a wandering accordion player. The tower's glass elevator promises spectacular views from the top (see p84).

Paris Las Vegas

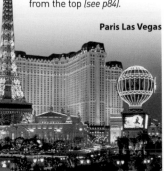

A DAY ON THE STRIP

Circus Circus
The Mirage Volcano
Forum Shops
Caesars Palace
Fountains of Bellagio
The Venetian
Flamingo Wildlife Habitat
Paris Las Vegas
New York-New York
Excalibur
Luxor
Mandalay Bay

▶ MORNING

Start with breakfast in the midst of Manhattan, at Il Fornaio bakery in **New York-New York**, then head south along the Strip, taking in the multicolored turrets of **Excalibur** (see p85) and the mighty pyramid of **Luxor** (see p81). Once you reach Mandalay Bay, be sure to visit the crocodiles in **Shark Reef Aquarium**.

Then head back north – it's quite a hike, so you may opt to take the Deuce bus (see p124) – to the **Flamingo Wildlife Habitat** (see p81). Now cross over to the Roman extravaganza of Caesars Palace, for lunch in the **Bacchanal Buffet** (see p70).

AFTERNOON

At the **Forum Shops at Caesars Palace** you may wish to shed the shoppers in your party.

Next stop is **The Venetian** (see p81), to be serenaded by operatic gondoliers on the Grand Canal, and enjoy a genuine Italian gelato in St. Mark's Square.

Another walk or bus ride will take you to **Circus Circus** (see p81) to catch free circus acts on the Midway or venture on the rides in the Adventuredome.

Once the sun goes down, savor two of the Strip's finest free spectacles. First watch the **Mirage Volcano** erupt, then continue to **Paris Las Vegas**, where excellent restaurants, including one within the replica Eiffel Tower, offer great views of the **Fountains of Bellagio** (see p81).

See map on p80 ←

Luxury Hotels

1 ARIA Resort and Casino
MAP Q1 ▪ 3730 Las Vegas Blvd S. ▪ 702 590 7111 ▪ www.aria.com ▪ $$$

As befits its location, this sleek CityCenter option is more of an upscale business hotel than a showpiece casino.

2 Bellagio
MAP Q1–2 ▪ 3600 Las Vegas Blvd S. ▪ 702 693 7111 ▪ www.bellagio.com ▪ $$$

Opulent Italianate hotel, with luxurious rooms curving around a gleaming lake, and an extravagant pool complex (see pp14–15).

Lobby of Caesars Palace

3 Caesars Palace
MAP P1 ▪ 3570 Las Vegas Blvd S. ▪ 866 227 2938 ▪ www.caesarspalace.com ▪ $$$

The rooms in this Roman palace – Vegas's definitive themed hotel – are more comfortable than ever.

4 The Cosmopolitan
MAP Q2 ▪ 3708 Las Vegas Blvd S. ▪ 702 698 7000 ▪ www.cosmopolitanlasvegas.com ▪ $$$

Large, very comfortable rooms with stylish modern furnishings; many have balconies overlooking the Bellagio fountains.

PRICE CATEGORIES

For a standard, double room per night (with breakfast if included), taxes, and extra charges.
....
$ under $100 $$ $100–200 $$$ over $200

---

5 The Cromwell
MAP P2 ▪ 3595 Las Vegas Blvd S. ▪ 702 777 3777 ▪ www.thecromwell.com ▪ $$$

The Strip's only "boutique hotel" offers 188 luxuriously appointed rooms.

6 Mandarin Oriental Las Vegas
MAP Q1 ▪ 3752 Las Vegas Blvd S. ▪ 702 590 8888 ▪ www.mandarin-oriental.com ▪ $$$

A stylish, non-gaming hotel situated at the heart of the Strip (see p25)

7 The Mirage
MAP P1–2 ▪ 3400 Las Vegas Blvd S. ▪ 702 791 7111 ▪ www.mirage.com ▪ $$

Las Vegas's original luxury resort, famous for its tropical atrium, pool, and Siegfried & Roy's white tigers.

8 Paris Las Vegas
MAP Q2 ▪ 3655 Las Vegas Blvd S. ▪ 877 796 2096 ▪ www.parislasvegas.com ▪ $$

Well-equipped central hotel, with plush rooms overlooking the Eiffel Tower and the Bellagio fountains.

9 The Venetian
MAP P2 ▪ 3355 Las Vegas Blvd S. ▪ 702 414 1000 ▪ www.venetian.com ▪ $$$

One of the world's largest hotels, the all-suite Venetian maintains consistently high standards (see pp16–17).

10 Wynn Las Vegas
MAP N2 ▪ 3131 Las Vegas Blvd S. ▪ 702 770 7000 ▪ www.wynnlasvegas.com ▪ $$$

This mega resort is the last word in Las Vegas luxury, with large and tasteful rooms (see pp18–19).

Affordable Hotels

1) Bally's
MAP Q2 ▪ 3645 Las Vegas Blvd S. ▪ 877 603 4390 ▪ www.ballyslasvegas.com ▪ $
Spacious, good-value rooms in a very central location, sharing access to the amenities of the fancier Paris Las Vegas next door.

2) Circus Circus
MAP M–N2 ▪ 2880 Las Vegas Blvd S. ▪ 702 734 0410 ▪ www.circuscircus.com ▪ $
This vast property, crammed with child-friendly attractions, offers rock-bottom rates and even has the only RV park on the Strip.

3) Excalibur
MAP R1 ▪ 3850 Las Vegas Blvd S. ▪ 702 597 7777 ▪ www.excalibur.com ▪ $
A longtime favorite with budget-conscious families and tour groups, this child's-drawing castle has some surprisingly pleasant rooms.

4) The Flamingo
MAP P2 ▪ 3555 Las Vegas Blvd S. ▪ 702 733 3111 ▪ www.flamingolasvegas.com ▪ $$
The oldest of the Strip's legendary casinos is now a mid-range property that offers some great rates.

5) Harrah's
MAP P2 ▪ 3475 Las Vegas Blvd S. ▪ 800 214 9110 ▪ www.harrahsvegas.com ▪ $
Friendly hotel with comfortable rooms, targeted at older visitors.

Exterior of Harrah's

Bedroom in The LINQ

6) The LINQ
MAP P2 ▪ 3535 Las Vegas Blvd S. ▪ 800 634 6441 ▪ www.caesars.com/linq ▪ $
The former Imperial Palace, now the centerpiece of an entertainment district, is one the Strip's best bargains.

7) Luxor
MAP R1 ▪ 3900 Las Vegas Blvd S. ▪ 702 262 4000 ▪ www.luxor.com ▪ $
Only in Las Vegas can you sleep in a glass-walled room in a 30-story pyramid overlooking a giant sphinx.

8) SLS Las Vegas
MAP M3 ▪ 2535 Las Vegas Blvd S. ▪ 702 761 7757 ▪ www.slslasvegas.com ▪ $
The former Sahara, now a mid-range hotel, is well positioned for Downtown as well as the Strip.

9) The Stratosphere
MAP M3 ▪ 2000 Las Vegas Blvd S. ▪ 702 380 7777 ▪ www.stratospherehotel.com ▪ $
Though the rooms aren't in its 1,000-ft (304-m) tower, the Stratosphere offers excellent value. For a great view with an adrenaline rush, pay for one of the rides at the top.

10) TI (Treasure Island)
MAP N2 ▪ 3300 Las Vegas Blvd S. ▪ 702 894 7111 ▪ www.treasureisland.com ▪ $
Treasure Island has come down to earth, abandoned its old pirate theme, and now cannily targets price-conscious blue-collar visitors.

See map on p80 ←

Places to Eat

Costa di Mare

1 Costa di Mare
MAP N2 ■ Wynn Las Vegas, 3131 Las Vegas Blvd S. ■ 702 770 3305 ■ $$$

Forty varieties of Mediterranean seafood are flown in daily for Mark LoRusso's nightly menu of expertly prepared Italian coastal cuisine. Dine outside in a lagoon-side cabana.

2 Bouchon Bistro
Classical French-bistro cuisine prepared using the season's finest ingredients is served in this casual yet elegant dining room. Added bonuses include a raw seafood bar, exquisite desserts, fine wines, and full bar service (see p67).

3 Picasso
The menu's modern cuisine is inspired by the regional dishes of France and Spain, where renowned artist Picasso lived. There is a fine European wine list, and a small, seasonal outdoor patio (see p66).

4 L'Atelier de Joël Robuchon
Enjoy the show with front-row seats at the counter facing the open kitchen where chef Jimmy Lisnard creates exquisite French-inspired tapas and tasting menus (see p66).

5 Michael Mina
MAP Q1–2 ■ Bellagio, 3600 Las Vegas Blvd S. ■ 702 693 7223 ■ $$$
High-quality ingredients and the fusion of Japanese and French flavors are integral to Mina's cuisine.

6 Cleo
MAP M3 ■ SLS Las Vegas, 2535 Las Vegas Blvd S. ■ 702 761 7612 ■ $$
Contemporary Mediterranean cuisine served in a sleek Cleopatra-themed setting. Chef Danny Elmaleh's signature dishes are kebabs, tagines, and moussaka.

7 Border Grill at Forum Shops
MAP P1–2 ■ The Forum Shops at Caesars, 3500 Las Vegas Blvd S. ■ 702 854 6700 ■ $$
Chefs Mary Sue Milliken and Susan Feniger, stars of Food Network's *Too Hot Tamales*, present Mexican cuisine and handcrafted cocktails.

8 Restaurant Guy Savoy
MAP P1–2 ■ Caesars Palace, 3570 Las Vegas Blvd S. ■ 702 731 7110 ■ $$$
Celebrated chef Guy Savoy's New French cuisine is prepared with the finest ingredients. An impressive list of cognacs is also available.

9 Sage
MAP P1–2 ■ ARIA, 3730 Las Vegas Blvd S. ■ 877 230 2742 ■ $$$
Contemporary American cuisine with global influences, crafted from farm-to-table produce. The emphasis is on seasonal ingredients and simple flavors to create imaginative fare.

10 SW Steakhouse
MAP N2 ■ Wynn Las Vegas, 3131 Las Vegas Blvd S. ■ 702 770 3305 ■ $$$
Steaks of outstanding Kobe beef, as well as fine seafood and vegan entrées, are flawlessly served in the elegant dining room or on the patio facing the Lake of Dreams.

Places to People-Watch

1 Bellagio Lobby
MAP Q1–2 ▪ Bellagio,
3600 Las Vegas Blvd S.
Settle down on a sofa to watch the gold dripping from the jet set. Soothe your envy with piano music from the caviar bar, Petrossian, and the marvelous artistry of the ceiling.

2 Fountains at Miracle Mile Shops
MAP Q2 ▪ Planet Hollywood,
3667 Las Vegas Blvd S.
When shopping gets tiring, sit down near the fountain in the heart of the Miracle Mile Shops at Planet Hollywood, and watch the illuminated fountain show set to original music.

3 Around the Casino Tables
The stars play at upscale casinos such as the MGM Grand, The Cosmopolitan, Bellagio, and Caesars Palace; stargazers should aim, apparently, for 11pm to 1am on weekends.

4 Mon Ami Gabi
MAP Q2 ▪ Paris Las Vegas
Hotel, 3655 Las Vegas Blvd S.
Take a table at the sidewalk café, soak up the atmosphere, and enjoy the view of Bellagio's fountain show.

5 Footbridges along the Strip
MAP N–R2
You can hop across Las Vegas Boulevard without playing traffic roulette, and enjoy marvelous vantage points of the thronging mêlée below.

6 Bodies… The Exhibition
MAP R1 ▪ Luxor Hotel & Casino, 3900 Las Vegas Blvd S.
Explore the beauty of the human body. This exhibit at Luxor (see p81) is dedicated to illustrating the wonders of our bodies and will inspire curiosity.

7 The Park
MAP Q1 ▪ 3782 Las Vegas Blvd S.
With its numerous restaurants, bars, and entertainment venues, The Park is a great place to enjoy a meal or a concert, or to simply spend time people-watching.

8 Fiber-Optic Signs
MAP R2 ▪ MGM Grand,
3799 Las Vegas Blvd S.
An incresing number of supersize signs like the one at MGM are appearing on the Strip. Expect to see vivid, lifelike clips of performers and upcoming attractions.

9 Third Floor of The Cosmopolitan
MAP Q1–2 ▪ 3708 Las Vegas Blvd S.
Take a seat in one of the comfy chairs near the pool table and watch people as they come and go from the resort's restaurants.

10 The Forum Shops at Caesars Palace
MAP P1–2 ▪ Caesars, 3570 Las Vegas Blvd S.
The cafés and benches within the shopping complex are as good for taking a break as they are for people-watching (see pp20–21).

The Forum Shops at Caesars Palace

See map on p80 ←

🔟 Downtown

Downtown Las Vegas is not a place of multi-story financial temples as is the case in most US cities. Instead, it is a conglomeration of government buildings, carnival attractions, not-so-very-glamorous casinos, and shops dealing in souvenirs and unclaimed pawn-shop miscellany. The heart of the area – the pedestrianized and LED-canopied Fremont Street – has a neon-lit row of iconic casinos, bars, restaurants, and, since the mid-1990s, free nightly entertainment in the form of a dazzling light-and-sound show, the Fremont Street Experience. This nightlife zone is here to stay, but a large-scale revitalization effort has also turned Downtown Las Vegas into a growing center for the arts and culture.

Stratosphere Tower

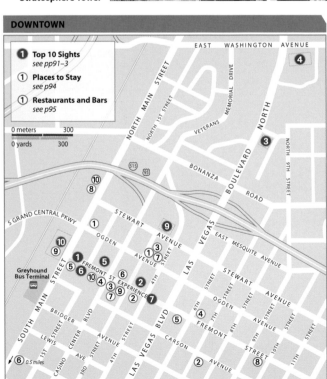

DOWNTOWN

- ① **Top 10 Sights**
  see pp91–3
- ① **Places to Stay**
  see p94
- ① **Restaurants and Bars**
  see p95

Previous pages The skyline of the Strip at twilight

1 Downtown's Neon Lights

This area encompasses about eight blocks that front on Fremont Street, between Main and Fourth streets. Along this stretch is the most concentrated dazzle of neon on the planet. Not only are all the Fremont Street casino fronts decorated with neon, but the street signs and light shows above also contribute to the sparkling brilliance. Nighttime, of course, is when the lighting is at its most intense. The crowds on the malled walkway are heavy until after midnight, and the entertainment adds to a feeling of carnival (see pp22–3).

2 Fremont Street Experience

MAP K4 ▪ Fremont St between Main and 4th

The Fremont Street Experience encompasses an LED display canopy that is 1,500 ft (457 m) long, zip lines that are strung beneath the screen, and a pedestrian promenade. It comes alive at night with light and sound shows, and live entertainment (see p22). Special events take place throughout the year, such as the St. Patrick's Day Celebration in March, Pride Parade in September, and a Veterans Day Parade in November.

Neon signs at the Neon Museum

3 Neon Museum

MAP K4 ▪ 770 Las Vegas Blvd S. ▪ 702 387 6366 ▪ Tours only ▪ www. neonmuseum.org ▪ Admission charge

Although the very name of Las Vegas remains synonymous with glowing neon, many of the city's finest signs have vanished from its streets. The mission of the Neon Museum is to gather them up and preserve them. Take a tour of its "Boneyard" to see neon gems from the long-lost Silver Slipper and other legendary casinos.

4 Old Las Vegas Mormon Fort Historic State Park

MAP J5 ▪ 500 Washington Ave E. ▪ 702 486 3511 ▪ Open 8am–4:30pm Tue–Sat ▪ Admission charge

Mormons built this fort, along with a trading post in 1855, as a defense against local Native Americans (who in fact turned out to be peaceful). It is the oldest building of its type in Nevada, but of the original structures, only a small adobe building, which formed part of the stockade, now remains.

5 Downtown Casinos

Along with all the outdoor activity on Fremont Street, there's action inside the casinos, too. They may not be as glamorous as the big hotels on the Strip, but the Fremont Street and other Downtown clubs have more history – some date back to the 1940s. They are also known for their bargain meals and buffets.

LED canopy over Fremont Street

NEW YEAR'S EVE IN DOWNTOWN LAS VEGAS

Historically, Downtown has been the place favored by Las Vegas resident revelers for New Year's Eve. Each year since the advent of the Fremont Street Experience, the celebrations have become more elaborate with live music and other entertainment; food and beverages; a countdown to midnight; fireworks (**below**); and dancing in the streets. Of course, there are paper hats and noisemakers, too. However, unlike most Fremont Street happenings on all other days of the year, some of the New Year's Eve festivities are not free.

6 Vegas Vic Sign
MAP K4

■ 25 Fremont St

Erected in 1951, 40-ft- (12-m-) tall Vegas Vic is a survivor from the early casino days. In bygone times, not only did he smoke and wave but he also talked, saying "Howdy pardner, welcome to Las Vegas." Vic has now become a Las Vegas icon and the backdrop for thousands of visitors' photographs each year.

7 SlotZilla Zip Line
MAP K4 ■ Fremont St

■ 702 678 5780 ■ Open 1pm–1am Sun–Thu, 1pm–2am Fri & Sat ■ www.vegasexperience. com ■ Admission charge

From what is said to be the world's tallest slot machine, soaring high over Fremont Street,

daredevil riders can choose to be launched along one of two separate zip lines. The lower line consists of ski-lift-style chairs; on the higher line, you're strapped into a harness and fly headfirst above the revelers below along the entire length of the Fremont Street Experience.

8 Street Festivals
MAP K4 ■ First Fri, throughout Downtown

Downtown Las Vegas's growth and revitalization has resulted in a number of street festivals. In the Arts District, First Friday invites people to explore the galleries and meet the artists. Some of the popular street festivals held are the Great Vegas Festival of Beer in April and the Life is Beautiful festival of music, art, and food, held every September or October.

9 The Mob Museum
MAP J4 ■ 300 Stewart Ave

■ 702 229 2734 ■ Open 9am–9pm daily ■ www. the mobmuseum.org ■ Admission charge

Vegas's notorious history is on display at the old courthouse, one of the most historic buildings in town. In addition to exhibits specific to Las Vegas, the museum examines organized crime on a larger scale, with artifacts and true-life accounts. A number of weapons, wire-tapping tools, and crime scene photos are displayed side by side with insider accounts on some of the biggest names of organized crime. These include Al Capone, Ben Siegel, Frank Rosenthal, and Whitey Bulger. The museum also examines popular Mob myths, and explains what happens when notable figures retire, die, or go into

Vegas Vic Sign

Exhibit at The Mob Museum

the witness protection program. A brewery, distillery, and bar are scheduled to open in late 2017.

⑩ Plaza Hotel and Casino

MAP J4 ▪ 1 Main St ▪ 702 386 2110 ▪ www.plazahotelcasino.com

From Main Street, the Plaza may look like just another casino, but it sits on a historic spot. Built during the 1970s, the Plaza is located on the very site of the birthplace of Las Vegas, at the first Union Pacific Railroad Depot Station. The station is no longer there, but the original railroad tracks can still be seen on the back side of the property. The Plaza has the only bingo room in Downtown Las Vegas. Bingo sessions are every two hours, beginning at 11am and ending at 9pm.

Plaza Hotel & Casino

DOWNTOWN AFTER DARK

▶ LATE AFTERNOON

Begin your excursion in the mid- to late afternoon, with a visit to the **Neon Museum** *(see p91)*. Make sure you have booked yourself onto a tour.

Next, explore Las Vegas's history with a visit to **The Mob Museum**, which offers a peek into the criminal past of the city. Make plans in advance to ensure it is open.

For a special treat, try dining at one of the top restaurants in Downtown, such as **Vic & Anthony's Steakhouse** at the Golden Nugget Casino *(see p95)*, with its classy decor, or the romantic **Hugo's Cellar** at Four Queens *(see p95)*.

NIGHTTIME

After dinner, stroll along Fremont Street's pedestrian promenade, stopping to watch people on the zip lines overhead and the buskers performing on the street. If gaming's your pleasure, step inside the El Cortez Hotel's casino for vintage slots *(see p94)*.

Check out the casino at the **Plaza**, then wander down to Main Street Station. Pick up a brochure here with a map and list of treasures – including street lamps from Brussels and a portion of the Berlin Wall – that have been incorporated into the building's interesting decor.

Back at **Fremont Street Experience** *(p91)*, top off the night by watching the stunning light-and-sound show.

See map on p90 ←

Places to Stay

PRICE CATEGORIES
For a standard double room per night (with breakfast if included), including taxes, and extra charges.

$ under $100 $$ $100–200 $$$ over $200

1 California Hotel
MAP J4 ▪ 12 Ogden Ave E.
▪ 702 385 1222 ▪ www.thecal.com ▪ $
Just off Fremont Street, this small casino offers plain, good-value rooms, plus, thanks to Las Vegas's unlikely association with Hawaii, assorted Hawaiian restaurants and bars.

2 The D
MAP K4 ▪ 301 E. Fremont St
▪ 702 388 2400 ▪ www.thed.com ▪ $
Formerly known as Fitzgerald's, this stylish Downtown casino has been transformed to hold spacious modern guest rooms.

3 Downtown Grand
MAP J4 ▪ 206 N. Third St
▪ 702 719 5100 ▪ www.downtown grand.com ▪ $
The plush contemporary rooms and suites in Downtown's newest hotel, facing the Mob Museum two blocks from Fremont Street, are the best option for business travelers.

4 El Cortez
MAP K4 ▪ 600 E. Fremont St
▪ 702 385 5200 ▪ www.elcortezhotel casino.com ▪ $
Long a byword for budget accommodation, El Cortez is a real throwback to vintage Vegas, with some attractive suites as well as rock-bottom standard rooms.

5 Golden Gate
MAP J4 ▪ 1 E. Fremont St
▪ 702 385 1906 ▪ www.goldengate casino.com ▪ $
The oldest hotel in Las Vegas, founded across from the brand-new railroad station in 1906, is now a self-styled "boutique hotel" with small but appealingly quirky rooms.

6 The Fremont Hotel
MAP K4 ▪ 200 E. Fremont St
▪ 702 385 3232 ▪ www. fremontcasino.com ▪ $
One of Downtown's classier options, in the heart of the Fremont Street Experience, with attractive rooms.

7 Four Queens
MAP K4 ▪ 202 E. Fremont St
▪ 702 385 4011 ▪ www.four queens.com ▪ $
Old-fashioned Downtown casino, where rather ordinary motel-style rooms are available at bargain rates.

8 Main Street Station
MAP J4 ▪ 200 N. Main St
▪ 702 387 1896 ▪ www.mainstreet casino.com ▪ $
Good-value casino/hotel, close to Fremont St, with decor designed to evoke New Orleans in the 1890s.

9 The Plaza
MAP J4 ▪ 1 Main St ▪ 702 386 2110 ▪ www.plazahotelcasino.com ▪ $
Large hotel in the long-defunct rail station, with some of Downtown's hippest bars and restaurants.

10 Golden Nugget
MAP K4 ▪ 129 E. Fremont St
▪ 702 385 7111 ▪ www.golden nugget.com ▪ $$
The only Downtown hotel that matches the Strip for luxury and amenities is a self-contained resort, with spectacular outdoor pool.

Golden Nugget

Restaurants and Bars

PRICE CATEGORIES

For a three-course meal for one with half a bottle of wine (or equivalent meal), taxes, and extra charges.

$ under $30 $$ $30–60 $$$ over $60

1 Freedom Beat

MAP J4 ▪ Downtown Grand, 206 N. Third St ▪ 702 719 5100 ▪ www.downtowngrand.com ▪ $

Created by chef Scott Commings, the menu takes diners on a culinary road trip – from Wisconsin to Texas to Colorado.

2 Eat

MAP K4 ▪ 707 Carson Ave ▪ 702 534 1515 ▪ www.eatdtlv.com ▪ $

Smart modern diner, a block off Fremont Street, serving flavorful break-fasts and light lunches.

3 Hugo's Cellar

MAP K4 ▪ Four Queens, 202 E. Fremont St ▪ 702 385 4011 ▪ www.fourqueens.com ▪ $$$

Much-loved on the Downtown dining scene, Hugo's is a special-occasion place offering romantic private booths and a classic menu of rich meat and seafood dishes.

4 Vic & Anthony's Steakhouse

MAP K4 ▪ Golden Nugget, 129 E. Fremont St ▪ 702 386 8399 ▪ www.vicandanthonys.com ▪ $$$

Old-fashioned steakhouse in Downtown's fanciest casino serving expensive but delicious prime cuts of beef and veal.

5 Beauty Bar

MAP K4 ▪ 517 E. Fremont St ▪ 702 598 1965 ▪ www.thebeautybar.com

Downtown's coolest bar, decorated as a vintage beauty salon, is a gathering place for local hipsters.

6 Lola's: A Louisiana Kitchen

MAP L3 ▪ 201 W. Charleston Ave ▪ 702 227 5652 ▪ www.lolaslasvegas.com ▪ $$

Authentic New Orleans-style bistro, one mile from Fremont Street on the southwestern edge of Downtown, serving a menu of Cajun and Creole favorites from shrimp and gumbo to grits and hush puppies.

7 Furnace Bar

MAP J4 ▪ Downtown Grand, 206 N. Third St ▪ 702 719 5100 ▪ www.downtowngrand.com ▪ $

Comfortable bar just off the hotel lobby, decorated with crystal chandeliers and ideal for an early-evening cocktail before hitting the casinos.

Eat

8 Atomic Liquors

MAP K5 ▪ 917 Fremont St ▪ 702 982 3000 ▪ www.atomicvegas.com

Established in 1952, the city's oldest free-standing bar, where rooftop drinkers once watched distant atomic tests, has been meticulously restored. The Rat Pack and Barbra Streisand were regulars.

9 Chicago Brewing Co.

MAP K4 ▪ Four Queens, 202 E. Fremont St ▪ 702 924 5222 ▪ www.fourqueens.com

Las Vegas isn't known for its brewpubs, so it's hardly surprising the craft beers at this lively spot, with views of the Downtown lights, draw crowds every night.

10 Triple Seven Restaurant and Microbrewery

MAP J4 ▪ Main Street Station, 200 N. Main St ▪ 702 387 1896 ▪ www.mainstreetcasino.com ▪ $

Huge pub/restaurant, open almost around the clock, and serving decent food along with its selection of house-brewed and imported beers.

See map on p90 ←

🔟 Beyond the Neon

Look beyond the neon and you will find that Las Vegas is, like the Roman god Janus, a two-faced town. One is about make-up and make-believe; the other is like that of other American towns, with popular city parks, a thriving university, community centers, and playgrounds. Las Vegas is a city where significant research is undertaken at medical centers, and where cultural performances take place almost every night. It is also a growing city of surprising diversity, with many ethnic neighborhoods and distinct areas.

UNLV Campus

BEYOND THE NEON

1 Chinatown Plaza
MAP B–C4 ▪ 4255 Spring Mountain Rd

With pagoda-style roofs, a traditional Chinese entrance gate, and a statue of the mythical monk Tripitaka, with his companions – a pig, a soldier, and a monkey – Chinatown Plaza offers a delightful blend of East and West. Stores specialize in both American and Eastern necessities and Asian luxuries. Chinese music wafts through the covered walkways, and art throughout the Plaza spotlights Chinese customs and traditions. Not surprisingly, this is the place to come for the best Asian cuisine in town. There are a number of Filipino, Korean, Japanese, and Vietnamese restaurants, in addition to the Chinese establishments.

Chinatown Plaza

2 Broadacres Marketplace & Event Center
MAP D2 ▪ 2390 Las Vegas Blvd N.

This swap meet brings together more than 1,150 vendors selling antiques, toys, crafts, shoes, and electronics. Although most items are priced, feel free to bargain for a better deal. On weekends, live bands play on a large stage with a covered seating area. The food options are plentiful, with stalls selling everything from burritos to barbecue fare.

3 UNLV Campus
MAP Q4 ▪ S. Maryland Parkway

City residents' favorite areas for taking a walk include the campus of the University of Nevada Las Vegas, which was established in 1957. The university may not have any remarkable buildings, but there are shady trees, and in early evening the paths are blissfully uncrowded. Be sure not to miss the lovely desert garden. Summer days are much warmer than winter days, but the campus is less crowded in the summer.

4 Dig This
MAP N1 ▪ 3012 Rancho Dr ▪ 702 222 4344 ▪ www.digthisvegas.com

For those who have always wanted to experience working in construction, this heavy equipment playground is a dream. Choose a bulldozer or excavator, go through an orientation exercise, then participate in one of the many activities such as building mounds, stacking tires, and digging deep trenches. Book in advance. Visitors must be over 8 years old and at least 48 in (122 cm) tall.

5 Ethel M Chocolate Factory

MAP E5 ■ 2 Cactus Garden Drive, Henderson ■ 702 435 2655 ■ Open 8am–8pm daily ■ www.ethelm.com

Take a free tour to view the glass-enclosed, spotless, white kitchens where the diligent candy-makers concoct their sweet creations. Find out what the large stainless steel machines do, and admire the finished confections wrapped in their foil of emerald, ruby, sapphire, and other jewel colors. Every participant receives a free chocolate at the end of the tour. Outside the factory is a lovely cactus garden, with plants clearly identified.

6 Las Vegas Motor Speedway

MAP E1 ■ 7000 Las Vegas Blvd N. ■ 702 644 4444 ■ Call for opening times

Completed in 1996, the 142,000-seat Las Vegas Motor Speedway was the first super-speedway to be built in the southwest USA in more than two decades. The 1,600-acre (647-ha) facility has 14 different race tracks, food courts, three levels of open-air grandstand viewing, VIP party rooms, and 102 luxury skybox suites. Important races staged here include NASCAR and National Hot Rod Association (NHRA) events. Visitors can take a lesson in race car driving

CASINOS BEYOND THE NEON

Although for the past few decades Las Vegas has been a sprawling city with shopping centers and clusters of businesses in the various neighborhoods, almost all of the hotel/casinos were concentrated in two areas – Downtown and along the Strip. In the 1980s, when the city's population began its explosive growth, a number of neighborhood hotel/casinos were built. Visitors who venture beyond the neon for gaming may be pleasantly surprised to find a friendly atmosphere and lovely surroundings (see p102).

from instructors at the Richard Petty Driving Experience. Concerts are sometimes held here as well, as is the annual Electric Daisy Carnival.

7 Henderson Farmers Market

200 S. Green Valley Pkwy, Henderson ■ 702 579 9661 ■ Open 9am–4pm Fri (Spring–early Fall)

Henderson's market had its beginnings in 1999 and gets bigger each season. Farmers drive from the California valleys to sell their produce year-round; in the summer season, they're joined by Nevada growers. Artisans sell everything from hand-painted china and rag dolls to house plants and chess sets.

NASCAR race at Las Vegas Motor Speedway

8 Voodoo Zipline

MAP P1 ■ Rio All-Suite Hotel & Casino, 3700 W. Flamingo Rd ■ 702 388 0477 ■ Open 11am–midnight daily ■ www.voodoozipline.com ■ Admission charge

The Rio's latest attraction consists of an absolutely terrifying thrill ride, on which riders race along a slender cable strung 500 ft (150 m) off the ground, with stunning city views. Mercifully, it's more like a ski lift than a traditional zip line, with each capsule holding two passengers.

Rio's hair-raising Voodoo Zipline

9 Sunset Park

MAP D5 ■ 2601 E. Sunset Rd

One of the city's most popular parks, Sunset offers basketball and tennis courts, and jogging tracks; a place to fly kites and sail boats; and some of the best picnic spots in town. It also has a well-kept dog park, popular with local dog walkers.

10 Marjorie Barrick Museum

MAP Q4 ■ UNLV campus ■ 702 895 3381 ■ Open 9am–5pm Mon–Wed & Fri; 9am–8pm Thu; noon–5pm Sat ■ Free (contributions suggested)

This small museum's collection focuses on modern art alongside Native American artefacts. It also contains exhibits exploring the area's natural history, anthropology and archaeology.

TWO EXCURSIONS BEYOND THE NEON

▶ MORNING EXCURSION

Begin with an early-morning stroll around the UNLV campus, stopping for a quick visit to the Marjorie Barrick Museum.

Drive to **Town Square Las Vegas** *(see p73)* where, if children are in your party, the play equipment will be the main attraction. Don't miss the shops while you're there. Then it's on to the **Ethel M Chocolate Factory** for the free tour and a walk around the cactus garden. Buy some chocolate for a local souvenir.

Before lunch, head to **Broadacres Marketplace** (open weekends only) for eclectic shopping and people watching, then stop by **Chinatown Plaza** for a bite to eat from one of the many Asian restaurants *(see p97)*.

AFTERNOON EXCURSION

Begin the afternoon excursion at the **Nevada State Museum and Historical Society** *(see p46)* to learn more about the Silver State. Motor-racing fans should then make their next stop the **Las Vegas Motor Speedway**.

Those who want to try their hand at driving heavy equipment should stop by **Dig This** *(see p97)* for an exhilarating and unique experience. If you have any energy left, **Sunset Park** is a great place to take a run or some time to relax if you prefer. Other outdoor areas offer opportunities for disc golf, hiking, and cycling. In the evening, visit a "locals casino" away from the Strip for a different dining and gaming experience *(see p102)*.

See map on pp96–7

Family Restaurants

1 Fatburger
MAP R2 ▪ 4663 E. Sunset Rd
(and other locations) ▪ 702 547 5535
▪ $

Big, handmade burgers, hearty fries, and a classic 1950s atmosphere make Fatburger a top Las Vegas hamburger destination. A classic rock-and-roll jukebox adds a note of authenticity and old-fashioned charm to the decor.

PRICE CATEGORIES
For a three course meal for one with a half bottle of wine (or equivalent meal), taxes, and extra charges.
....
$ under $30 $$ $30–60 $$$ over $60

1950s-style burger joint, Fatburger

2 BJ's Restaurant & Brewhouse
10840 W. Charleston Ave ▪ 702 853 2300 ▪ $

Salads, sandwiches, pastas, and steaks, but the main draw is the pizzas. Great lunch specials.

3 Buca di Beppo
MAP Q3 ▪ 412 E. Flamingo Rd
▪ 702 866 2867 ▪ $$

There are family-style platters and hefty bottles of wine to be had at this authentic Italian dining experience.

4 Omelet House
MAP L2 ▪ 2160 W. Charleston Blvd ▪ 702 384 6868 ▪ $

This low-key breakfast spot serves the under-10 crowd meals big enough to satisfy an adult.

5 Wienerschnitzel
MAP E4 ▪ 4680 E. Flamingo Rd
(and other locations) ▪ 702 362 0418
▪ $

Drive-thru hotdog stand, with both the traditional dogs and variations.

6 Romano's Macaroni Grill
MAP C3 ▪ 2400 W. Sahara
▪ 702 248 9500 ▪ $

Bruschetta, fried mozzarella cheese, Italian panini sandwiches, and mouth-watering pasta.

7 Lotus of Siam
MAP M4 ▪ 953 E. Sahara Ave
▪ 702 735 3033 ▪ $$

One of the finest Thai restaurants in Vegas, known for its excellent service.

8 Mimi's Café
6790 N. Durango Dr ▪ 702 645 3688 ▪ $

Comfort food served in a warm atmosphere. Portions are large.

9 LYFE Kitchen
MAP E6 ▪ 140 S. Green Valley Pkwy ▪ 702 558 0131 ▪ $

A modern, healthy eatery next to the Green Valley Ranch Resort with many vegetarian and vegan options.

10 Original Pancake House
4170 S. Fort Apache Rd
▪ 702 433 5800 ▪ $

The portions are huge; the pancakes, divine. And so many varieties – blueberry, apple, plate-size German pancakes, or buttermilk hotcakes as small as silver dollars.

Original Pancake House

Bars and Nightlife

Stained-glass ceiling at Gaudi Bar

1 Gaudi Bar
MAP F6 ■ Sunset Station, 1301 W. Sunset Rd ■ 702 547 7777 ■ Open 24hr daily ■ www.sunsetstation.sclv.com

Las Vegas's most extraordinary casino bar. This cavernous space, studded with mosaics and tiles, was designed and named in honor of Spanish architect Antoni Gaudí.

2 Double Down Saloon
MAP Q3 ■ 4640 Paradise Rd ■ 702 791 5775 ■ Open 24hr daily ■ www.doubledown saloon.com

Tiny dive bar near the Hard Rock Hotel, with street art murals, pool tables, and live punk, ska, and psychobilly bands nightly.

3 Flex Cocktail Lounge
MAP B3 ■ 4371 W. Charleston Blvd ■ 702 878 3355 ■ Open 24hr daily ■ www.flex lasvegas.com

Free nightly entertainment every night of the week at this legendary gay bar, including famous late-night drag shows on Thursday and Saturday. Daily specials too.

4 Crown & Anchor
MAP R5 ■ 1350 E. Tropicana Ave ■ 702 739 8676 ■ Open 24hr daily ■ www.crownand anchorlv.com

This English-style sports pub in the university district is the place for watching live soccer, showing games from around the world. Traditional pub food is served 24 hours a day.

5 The Garage
MAP Q3 ■ 51487 E. Flamingo Rd ■ 702 440 6333 ■ Open 24hr daily

Welcoming neighborhood gay bar with a mechanic theme that will appeal to car enthusiasts.

6 Herbs & Rye
MAP C3 ■ 3713 W. Sahara Ave ■ 702 982 8036 ■ Open 5pm–3am Mon–Sat ■ www.herbsandrye.com

Cocktail lounge and tapas bar that evokes the spirit of a Prohibition-era speakeasy, with classic cocktails.

7 Stoney's Rockin' Country
MAP C5 ■ 6611 Las Vegas Blvd S. ■ 702 435 2855 ■ Open 7pm–2am Wed–Sat ■ www.stoneysrockin country.com

The city's biggest and wildest country bar puts on everything from line dancing to bikini bull riding.

8 Mermaid Bar & Lounge
MAP C6 ■ Silverton Casino, 3333 Blue Diamond Rd ■ 702 263 7777 ■ Open 11–1am daily ■ www.silvertoncasino.com

This casino lounge lives up to its name – its aquarium tank is not only filled with fish but features water ballets by real (almost!) mermaids.

9 Piranha
MAP Q3 ■ 4633 Paradise Rd ■ 702 379 9500 ■ Open 10pm–5am Sun–Thu, 10pm–6am Fri–Sat ■ www.piranhavegas.com

Las Vegas's most spectacular gay nightclub, the epicenter of the so-called "Fruit Loop," offers an adjoining ultra lounge for VIPs.

10 The Railhead
MAP E4 ■ Boulder Station, 4111 Boulder Hwy ■ 702 547 5300 ■ Opening times vary ■ www.boulderstation.sclv.com

Lounge showroom in a lively neighborhood casino, with a varied program of rock, blues, and tribute bands, as well as dance nights.

See map on pp96–7

Casinos

Green Valley Ranch Resort

1 Green Valley Ranch Resort
2300 Paseo Verde Parkway, Henderson ▪ 702 617 7777

Inspired by the great casinos of Europe, upscale Green Valley Ranch has over 2,000 slot and video poker machines and 55 table games.

2 Rampart Casino
MAP A3 ▪ 221 N. Rampart Blvd ▪ 702 869 7777

An intimate gaming atmosphere with a relaxing, upscale casino floor away from the crowds of the Strip.

3 Santa Fe Station
MAP A1 ▪ 4949 N. Rancho Drive ▪ 800 678 2846

Mid-size gambling floor (2,900 slots) and many entertainment options, the Santa Fe is patronized primarily by locals and is one of the more pleasant casinos beyond the neon.

4 Rio All-Suite Hotel & Casino
MAP P1 ▪ 3700 W. Flamingo Rd ▪ 888 396 2483

Home of the World Series of Poker, the Rio has more video machines than most, and a friendly feeling associated with casinos that rely on local trade for repeat business.

5 Fiesta Rancho
MAP B2 ▪ 2400 N. Rancho Drive ▪ 702 631 7000

From cocktail waitresses in jewel-toned satin outfits to the gaily patterned carpets on the floor, this budget, Mexican-themed casino evokes party time.

6 Texas Station
MAP B2 ▪ 2101 N. Rancho Drive ▪ 702 631 1000

The theme is of a 19th-century town in the Lone Star state of Texas, with wagon wheels and gunpowder barrels around the gaming floor.

7 Sunset Station
MAP F6 ▪ 1301 W. Sunset Rd, Henderson ▪ 702 547 7777

Mediterranean-themed casino with wrought-iron balconies. Natural light makes it more pleasant than most.

8 Sam's Town
MAP E4 ▪ 5111 Boulder Hwy, Las Vegas ▪ 702 456 7777

One of the largest non-Strip casinos with thousands of slots, video poker, and keno machines.

9 The Orleans
MAP B4 ▪ 4500 W. Tropicana Ave ▪ 702 365 7111

There's a feeling of Mardi Gras in this casino, which is patterned after New Orleans' Vieux Carré.

10 Arizona Charlie's
MAP B3 ▪ 740 S. Decatur Blvd ▪ 702 258 5200

Dude-ranch theme touches include deer antler chandeliers. Pai Gow Poker and Royal Match 21 are included in the games.

Shopping

1 Chinatown Plaza
A shopping center that serves the needs of the city's sizable Asian community as well as visitors from around the world. At festival times (see p76), counters are piled high with moon cakes and treats linked to special days (see also p97).

2 Bonanza Gift Shop
MAP M3 ▪ 2440 Las Vegas Blvd S.
The store claims to be the largest gift shop in the world, with souvenirs ranging from T-shirts to the iconic green dealer's visors.

3 Antique Mall of America
9151 Las Vegas Blvd S.
More than 100 booths selling an eclectic mix of antiques, collectibles, jewelry, art, furniture, and much more.

4 Las Vegas Premium Outlets
MAP C6 ▪ 7400 Las Vegas Blvd S.
A truly fabulous place for any shoppers in your party who may have "champagne" tastes but "house-wine" wallets.

5 Cost Plus World Market
MAP A2 ▪ 2151 N. Rainbow Blvd
Large American retail chain with handsome tableware, furniture, food-stuffs, and art objects from all corners of the world at discount prices.

6 Fantastic Indoor Swap Meet
MAP B3 ▪ 1717 S. Decatur Blvd ▪ Open 10am–6pm Fri–Sun
The swap meet is the American equivalent of the European flea market: vintage kitchen appliances, tire chains, home-baked bread, mismatched chairs, etc.

7 Bass Pro Shops
MAP C6 ▪ 8200 Dean Martin Dr
Located at the Silverton Casino, this reliable chain is known for its wide array of hunting, fishing, and outdoor gear.

8 Total Wine & More
730 Rampart Blvd
A massive store featuring 8,000 wines, 3,000 spirits, and 2,500 beers. The staff are very knowledgeable.

9 Fry's Electronics
MAP C5 ▪ 6845 Las Vegas Blvd S.
Situated at the south end of the Town Square mall, this is the largest electronics store in Las Vegas.

10 Desert Outfitters
MAP N1 ▪ 3340 W. Sirius Ave
This quirky shop supplies everything the wannabe Wild-West prospector might need, from pickaxes and sifting pans to outlines of ghost towns and abandoned mines.

The exterior of Bonanza Gift Shop

See map on pp96–7

TOP 10 Lake Mead, Hoover Dam, and Laughlin

Penstock towers, Hoover Dam

The Hoover Dam, most assuredly, changed the face of the American West. Not only did it enable the production of vast amounts of electrical energy and help to control floods, but it also provides water to cities and farms throughout the American Southwest and Mexico. The project's commercial byproducts in Nevada – Lake Mead and Boulder City, and the resort city of Laughlin – have infused billions of dollars into the state's economy and provided recreational opportunities for the hundreds of millions of visitors who come here every year.

LAKE MEAD, HOOVER DAM, AND LAUGHLIN

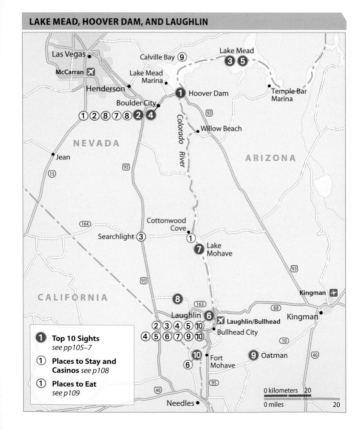

1 Top 10 Sights
see pp105–7

1 Places to Stay and
Casinos see p108

1 Places to Eat
see p109

Lake Mead National Recreation Area

1 Hoover Dam Tour

MAP T2 ■ Visitor Center, Hoover Dam ■ 702 494 2517 ■ Tour reservations 866 730 9097

Begin a visit in the three-story visitor center perched on the Nevada canyon wall. From here, Bureau of Reclamation guides offer tour options into the hydropower plant or the dam itself. Enjoy audio and film presentations, exhibits, and other media that tell the story of the Colorado River's settlement and the facts behind the technology involved in the distribution of water and production of hydroelectric power. Catch the view from the top of the center to see the face of the dam, Lake Mead behind, and the Colorado River below (see pp26–7).

2 Boulder City/ Hoover Dam Museum

MAP T2 ■ 1305 Arizona St, Boulder City ■ 702 294 1988 ■ Open 10am–5pm daily ■ Admission charge

Built in 1933, the Dutch Colonial-style Boulder Dam Hotel now houses the Boulder City/Hoover Dam Museum. Actor Boris Karloff and other Hollywood stars stayed here during the hotel's glory days, and Crown Prince Olav and Princess Martha of Norway hosted a party here in 1939. The out-of-town hotel's popularity declined in the postwar rise of Las Vegas as a tourist mecca, but, since the mid-1990s, a group of volunteers has set about rehabilitating it. The museum itself includes memorabilia from the city's early days in the 1930s (see pp26–7).

3 Lake Mead National Recreation Area

MAP U2 ■ Information from Alan Bible Visitor Center ■ 601 Nevada Way, Boulder City ■ 702 293 8990 ■ www. nps.gov/lake

After the completion of the Hoover Dam in 1935, the waters of the Colorado River filled the deep canyons that once towered above the river to create a huge reservoir. This lake, with its 550 miles (885 km) of shoreline, is the centerpiece of the 2,300-sq-mile (6,000-sq-km) Lake Mead National Recreation Area.

4 Boulder City Historic District

MAP T2 ■ Information from Hoover Dam Museum ■ Hwy 93 at Lakeshore Rd ■ 702 294 1988

It's worth including Boulder City on a Hoover Dam trip to appreciate the scale of work involved – the city was built to house dam construction workers. The grandest buildings are the Bureau of Reclamation and the Bureau of Light headquarter buildings; the Municipal Building; and the Boulder Dam Hotel.

Boulder City Historic District

Entrance to Lake Mead Marina

5 Lake Mead Marinas and Beaches

MAP U2 ▪ Information from Alan Bible Visitor Center ▪ 702 293 8990

Lake Mead's numerous marinas and beaches range from delightful tiny coves to long stretches of sand. Popular areas include Lake Mead RV Village, Echo Bay, Boulder Beach, Lake Mead Marina, and Temple Bar. These have recreational vehicle sites with full hookups, and supplies available from nearby stores. Boxcar and Icebox coves are favorites with houseboaters.

Petroglyphs near Laughlin

Callville Bay, Las Vegas Boat Harbor, and Lake Mead marinas are the closest ones to Hoover Dam, while Temple Bar marina serves the lake's southeasternmost reaches.

6 Laughlin's Casino Row

MAP T3 ▪ 90 miles (145 km) S. of Las Vegas ▪ www.visitlaughlin.com

The establishments lining Laughlin's South Casino Drive may not be as dazzling as those along the Las Vegas Strip, but they offer extremely good value. Getting around is easier than in Las Vegas: a riverwalk connects most of the casinos, or you can take a bus or shuttle boat. Tours of the Colorado River are also available.

7 Lake Mohave

MAP U2 ▪ Part of Lake Mead National Recreation Area
▪ www.nps.gov/lake
▪ Admission fee to park

The 67-mile- (108-km-) long lake extends from below Hoover Dam to Davis Dam, 2 miles (3.2 km) north of Laughlin, and is only 4 miles (6.4 km) across at its widest point. A National Park Service Visitor Center at Katherine Landing, just north of Laughlin, offers free guided walks by park rangers. Boat rentals and fishing tackle are available at Katherine Landing, Willow Beach Marina, and Cottonwood Cove. Record-size striped bass have been caught in Lake Mohave.

8 Petroglyphs near Laughlin

MAP T3 ▪ Part of Lake Mead National Recreation Area
▪ www.nps.gov/lake

Christmas Tree Pass and Grapevine Canyon, just west of Laughlin on Hwy 163, are the best places to see the fascinating petroglyphs incised into the cliffs of the canyons by the early

---

THE LAUGHLIN STORY

Don Laughlin opened his four-unit motel and bar with about a dozen slot machines on the banks of the Colorado River in the same week in 1966 as the opulent Caesars Palace opened in Las Vegas. Laughlin town (named by the postmaster in 1977) is now Nevada's third busiest gambling destination – outranked only by the major gaming centers of Las Vegas and Reno.

Patayan group. The line drawings and symbols may have served as the road maps of their day, directing hunters and fishermen. National Park Service personnel have located more than 150 Patayan camp sites between Davis Dam and Willow Beach, which is 10 miles (16 km) from the base of Hoover Dam.

9 Oatman, Arizona
MAP U3 ■ General information
928 768 6222

A century ago, Oatman was a thriving gold mining center; today, visitors are taken back to the old days of the Wild West, with burros roaming the streets and staged gunfights in the middle of town. The Oatman Hotel was where honeymooners Clark Gable and Carole Lombard stayed in 1939. The town has been used as the location for a number of movies, including *How the West Was Won*.

Donkeys on Main Street, Oatman

10 Avi Resort and Casino
MAP T3

In 1995, the Fort Mojave Indian tribe opened Nevada's first Native American-owned casino and the only Native American-owned gaming business in the USA operated under state regulations. "Avi" means money or loose change. The resort is in an area that the tribe intends to develop as a planned community (see also p108).

TWO DAYS AT THE DAM AND LAUGHLIN

▶ DAY ONE

Begin with early-morning coffee at **Railroad Pass Casino** on Hwy 93, an old-timer among gambling dens. Afterward, continue on Hwy 93 to the historic **Boulder City** and **Hoover Dam** *(see p105)* for the amazing tour.

Go back along Hwy 93 to the junction with Hwy 95 and turn south toward Laughlin. Stop at **Terrible's Roadhouse** *(see p109)* in Searchlight for lunch and the chance to visit a typical small-town Nevada casino.

For a more picturesque route, turn off 95 and head east on the dirt road through Christmas Tree Pass. Spend the remainder of the day in **Laughlin**, perhaps hunting for bargains at the 50-store Laughlin Outlet Center.

Stay overnight at **Harrah's** *(see p108)* or another hotel on the river, and be sure to take an evening stroll along its banks.

DAY TWO

Early next morning, golfers can tee off at any of the five area championship golf courses, where you can golf in two states (Nevada, and Arizona).

Later, head for **Oatman**, an old-time western town about a half-hour's drive southeast from Bullhead City. In the afternoon, drive back north to **Lake Mohave**. Be sure to make time to see the mysterious prehistoric **petroglyphs** at Grapevine Canyon, off Hwy 163, before returning to your hotel in Laughlin.

See map on p104 ←

Places to Stay and Casinos

1 Cottonwood Cove Resort & Marina

MAP U3 ▪ 10000 Cottonwood Cove Rd, Searchlight ▪ 702 297 1464 ▪ $$$

Houseboats in various sizes and with excellent facilities can be rented here. All you have to bring on deck is food, bedding, toiletries, and clothing.

2 Golden Nugget, Laughlin

MAP T3 ▪ 2300 S. Casino Drive ▪ 702 298 7111 ▪ $$

A tropical atrium with cascading waterfalls, palm trees, and 300 species of tropical plants sets this hotel apart. The casino, with its 24 Karat Slot Club, is also more attractive than most.

3 Don Laughlin's Riverside Resort, Laughlin

MAP T3 ▪ 1650 S. Casino Drive ▪ 702 298 2535 ▪ $

A total destination resort. Unusual features include two classic auto showrooms and a display of antique slot machines. There's also an RV park with full hookups.

4 Aquarius Casino Resort, Laughlin

MAP T3 ▪ 1900 S. Casino Drive ▪ 702 298 5111 ▪ $

The hotel features a large pool deck overlooking the river and Arizona hills, fitness center, a wedding chapel, and Laughlin's largest tour boat, the *Celebration*.

5 Colorado Belle, Laughlin

MAP T3 ▪ 2010 S. Casino Drive ▪ 702 298 4000 ▪ $

Overlooking the Colorado River, this resort is housed in a replica paddle-wheel boat and boasts the only microbrewery in Laughlin, Pints Brewery. Special events and musical perform-ances are staged on a regular basis.

PRICE CATEGORIES

For a standard, double room per night (with breakfast if included), including taxes, and extra charges.

....

$ under $100 $$ $100–200 $$$ over $200

6 Avi Resort and Casino, near Laughlin

MAP T3 ▪ 10,000 Aha Macav Parkway ▪ 702 535 5555 ▪ $

This Native American-owned resort *(see p107)* has a large, sandy, riverside beach, a video arcade, a swimming pool, live entertainment, and 29 spa suites.

7 Quality Inn, Boulder City

MAP T2 ▪ 110 Ville Drive ▪ 702 293 6444 ▪ $

This 70-room motor hotel features great views over Lake Mead.

8 El Rancho Boulder Motel, Boulder City

MAP T2 ▪ 725 Nevada Hwy ▪ 702 293 1085 ▪ $

Spanish-style motel on the main street. Some rooms have kitchens.

9 Callville Bay, Lake Mead

MAP T2 ▪ On the north side of Boulder Basin ▪ 702 565 8958 ▪ $

The campground offers showers, restrooms, a restaurant, lounge, and fuel. Reservations are not accepted.

10 Harrah's, Laughlin

MAP T3 ▪ 2900 S. Casino Drive ▪ 702 298 4600 ▪ $

Spanish-themed property with its own sand beach, a casino looking out on the river, five restaurants, and a particularly pleasant ambience.

Harrah's, Laughlin

Places to Eat

1 Boulder Dam Brewing Company, Boulder City
MAP T2 ■ 453 Nevada Hwy ■ 702 243 2739 ■ $

A family eatery serving fresh brews and great food. The walls are adorned with artifacts from the dam's construction. There is also a beer garden.

Boulder Dam Brewing Company

2 Toto's Mexican Restaurant, Boulder City
MAP T2 ■ 806 Buchanan Blvd ■ 702 293 1744 ■ $

Standard Mexican cuisine is done with flair at this popular chain.

3 Terrible's Roadhouse
MAP T2 ■ 100 Highway 95 ■ 702 297 1201 ■ $

This restaurant is dominated by a mural of the *Searchlight*, an 1880s riverboat. The signature dish is a jumbo corn muffin with sausage, scrambled eggs, and gravy.

4 The Steakhouse, Laughlin
MAP T3 ■ Tropicana Express Hotel and Casino, 2121 S. Casino Drive ■ 888 888 8695 ■ $$

Resembling a Victorian railroad parlor car, The Steakhouse has a romantic, intimate ambience and a contemporary dining menu.

5 Bighorn Café, Laughlin
MAP T3 ■ Laughlin River Lodge, 2700 S. Casino Drive ■ 800 835 7903 ■ $

Delicious American cuisine is served under open-beam ceilings and in front of a roaring fire.

6 Fresh Market Square Buffet, Harrah's, Laughlin
MAP T3 ■ 2900 S. Casino Drive ■ 702 298 4600 ■ $

A buffet offering six action stations where you can watch the food being cooked and themed areas including Mexican, sushi, Italian, seafood, and American.

7 Saltgrass Steak House, Laughlin
MAP T3 ■ 2300 S. Casino Drive ■ 702 298 7153 ■ $$

A popular steakhouse that regularly attracts a host of local families. The prices are affordable for the cowboy-themed dishes, such as the "Wagon Boss Top Sirloin" steak.

8 Milo's Cellar, Boulder City
MAP T2 ■ 538 Nevada Hwy ■ 702 293 9540 ■ $

This sidewalk café, wine bar, and liquor store serves a variety of gourmet sandwiches, antipasti, and cheese platters, as well as hundreds of wines and over 40 types of beer.

9 Bubba Gump Shrimp Company, Laughlin
MAP T3 ■ Golden Nugget, 2300 S. Casino Drive ■ 702 298 7143 ■ $

At this seafood restaurant you can choose between indoor seating with a casual atmosphere or outdoor seating under a covered patio.

10 The Prime Rib Room, Laughlin
MAP T3 ■ Riverside Casino, 1650 S. Casino Drive ■ 702 298 2535 ■ $

The specialty at this restaurant is prime rib, carved at your table. However, there are other entrées, including chicken and fish.

See map on p104

🔟 Parks and Preserves

Less than an hour from the man-made extravaganzas and simulations of the Strip are natural wonders so dramatic and thrilling that humans could not begin to replicate them. Many of these wonders are geological phenomena formed millions of years ago. The closest is the magnificent desert region of Red Rock Canyon *(see pp28–9)*. Also nearby are Zion National Park, with its fantastic rock formations, and Death Valley – the hottest place in the world – whose floor lies 282 ft (86 m) below sea level, making it the lowest elevation in the western hemisphere. Most famous is undoubtedly the Grand Canyon, whose size and appearance are breathtaking. Each region has its distinct flora and fauna, with a number of species that are found nowhere else on Earth.

Desert View Watchtower

PARKS AND PRESERVES

① **Top 10 Sights** see pp111–113	① **Natural Formations** see p117
① **Places to Stay** see p119	① **Hiking Trails** see p120
① **Places to Eat** see p118	

1 Kolob Canyons, Zion National Park

MAP U1 ■ Information from Kolob Canyons Visitor Center, just east of exit 40 off 1-15 north in Utah ■ 435 772 3256

The Kolob Canyons section offers viewpoints of steep canyons and a 5-mile (8-km) scenic drive. It also offers the closest access to Kolob Arch, which is one of the largest free-standing arches in the world.

2 Lost City Museum, Overton

MAP U2 ■ 721 S. Moapa Valley Blvd, Overton ■ 702 397 2193 ■ Open 8:30am–4:30pm daily ■ Admission charge

Artifacts salvaged from Pueblo Grande de Nevada – now known as Nevada's "Lost City" – before it was inundated by Lake Mead are displayed at this pueblo-style

Kolob Canyons, Zion National Park

museum opened in 1935. Exhibits include a village reconstruction, hunting weapons, and pottery.

3 Petroglyph Canyon, Valley of Fire

MAP U2 ■ 702 397 2088 ■ Admission charge for park

Petroglyph Canyon is the Valley of Fire's most popular attraction, carrying as it does the park's largest concentration of petroglyphs – symbols and drawings incised on the rock faces by prehistoric Native Americans from the Lost City. The purpose of the petroglyphs is unclear: some may have been no more than the road signs of their day, while others might have had a religious or mystical significance. The trail goes to Mouse's Tank.

4 Zion Canyon

MAP V1 ■ Information from Zion Canyon Visitor Center, Hwy 9, nr Springdale ■ 435 772 3256 ■ www.nps.gov/zion

A shuttle system takes visitors along the scenic drive to the Temple of Sinawava (closed to private vehicles from April to October). Of special interest are the Court of the Patriarchs, the Streaked Wall, and the Virgin River. The Zion-Mt Carmel Highway is also a spectacular drive. If you can stay, head for Zion Lodge (see also p119). Reserve a site early if you want to ensure a camping spot.

View from Bright Angel Point, North Rim, Grand Canyon

⑤ Bright Angel Point, North Rim, Grand Canyon

MAP V2 ■ North Rim Visitor Center, Bright Angel Peninsula ■ Open mid-May–mid-Oct

The North Rim of the Grand Canyon may be more remote than the South Rim, but it is worth the effort. From the North Rim Visitor Center, walk the 0.25-mile (0.4-km) trail to Bright Angel Point for canyon views.

⑥ Yavapai Geology Museum, South Rim, Grand Canyon

MAP V2 ■ 5 miles (8 km) N. of south entrance ■ Open 8am–8pm

For a visual introduction to Grand Canyon geology, you can scarcely beat the view from Yavapai Observation Station. Look down to the canyon floor for views of the Phantom Ranch and the Colorado River. The river flows along the bottom of the canyon, a little less than 5,000 ft (1,500 m) below the rim. From this great height it doesn't look very threatening, even with binoculars, but from the canyon floor it's a wildly impressive sight.

⑦ The Watchtower, Desert View, Grand Canyon

MAP V2 ■ On Hwy 64 at Desert View

A re-creation of an ancestral Puebloan tower, this landmark structure, designed by regional architect Mary Colter in 1932, is the highest point on the South Rim. The upper floor of the stone-built tower is decorated with Hopi murals. A gift store and refreshments are available. Other Colter designs at Grand Canyon include Hopi House, Hermits Rest, the Lookout Studio, and the cabins at Phantom Ranch.

⑧ Grand Canyon West

MAP U2 ■ 928 769 2636 ■ Open daily ■ www.grandcanyon west.com ■ Admission charge

This remote desert area, on the Hualapai Indian Reservation at the western end of the Grand Canyon, is the easiest part of the canyon to reach by air from Las Vegas. The car journey is long and along dirt roads. Besides the Skywalk, it offers tremendous canyon viewpoints and Western-themed attractions.

ANCIENT ROCKS

The Grand Canyon and Death Valley reveal more of the earth's geological history than anywhere else on the planet (some of its rocks are 1.7 billion years old). The mesas and cliffs of Zion National Park, too, were laid down and sculpted by the elements over millions of years. It is illegal to remove rocks or other artifacts from any national parks – if you do so, you may be fined.

9 Skywalk, Grand Canyon West

MAP U2 ▪ 928 769 2636 ▪ Open daily
▪ www.grandcanyonwest.com
▪ Admission charge

This iconic, horseshoe-shaped walkway, juts out from a red-rock clifftop above a 4,000-ft (1,200-m) drop at Grand Canyon West, and is best visited on a "flightseeing" day-trip. The gimmick, of course, is its see-through glass floor; it's perfectly safe, but you will need nerves of steel to take your first step.

10 Scotty's Castle, Death Valley

MAP S1 ▪ Hwy 267, at N. end of Death Valley ▪ 760 786 3280
▪ Closed for repair work
▪ Admission charge

Less of a castle and more of a Mediterranean-style mansion, the main man-made visitor attraction at Death Valley was built in the 1920s by the Chicago insurance magnate Albert Johnson. But Wild West show cowboy and conman Walter Scott had a habit of bragging that the spread was his, and it came to be called Scotty's Castle after him. A nice twist to the tale is that, in his last years, Scott was befriended by Johnson and spent his final years living at the coveted castle. Tours of the interior are available year round: fine craftsmanship is evident in the intricate wood carvings, wrought iron, and ornate tiling. Following a flood in 2015, the castle is closed – it should reopen in 2019.

Scotty's Castle, Death Valley

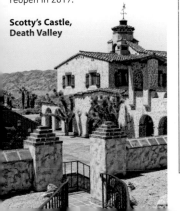

THREE TRIPS FROM VEGAS

It is not possible to do all trips in one day. Return to Las Vegas in between each place, making three separate excursions.

THE ROAD TO ZION

For an overnight trip to remember, drive east on Highway 15 to the turning for the Valley of Fire. Spend an hour or two on the park's scenic drive, hiking through **Petroglyph Canyon** (see p111) to **Mouse's Tank** (see p120) and visiting the **Lost City Museum** (see p111). Then, back on Highway 15, proceed to Mesquite for lunch, making sure you are within reach of one of Zion's many viewpoints by sunset: you will be richly rewarded. Spend the night camping in the park or at accommodation in Springdale.

GRAND CANYON

Take Highway 93 to Kingman, then Highways 40 and 64 to the national park. It is possible to view much of the canyon's natural grandeur by driving along the rim routes, but the total canyon experience involves hiking or riding to the valley floor, spending the night, and perhaps river-rafting. For insights into Native American culture, visit one of the reservations along the rim.

DEATH VALLEY

There are three major routes from Las Vegas to Death Valley. To choose the route most appropriate for your trip, visit www.nps.gov/deva for detailed information and planning tips. Bar food and spectacular scenery are available from Stovepipe Wells (see p118).

See map on pp110–11 ←

Local Flora and Fauna

1 Pine Forests

Dense forests of scrubby piñon pine, stunted by poor, dry soil, grow 6,500 ft (2,000 m) above sea level in the Grand Canyon (the canyon's highest elevation is 9,000 ft, or 2,750 m). About every seven years they produce bumper crops of edible nuts.

2 Wildflowers

Grand Canyon wildflowers include asters, sunflowers, globe mallows, and Indian paintbrushes. At Zion, look out for columbines, penstemons, Indian paintbrushes, and many varieties of sunflowers. Death Valley has fewer species, but Panamint daisies grow in profusion.

Indian paintbrushes

3 Sagebrush

The Nevada state flower is found up to 10,000 ft (3,000 m) above sea level and can grow as tall as 7 ft (2 m). These dense clusters of tiny yellow or cream flowers bloom in late summer.

4 Birds of Prey

Red-tailed hawks are the most common predatory birds in all three of the parks, but at the Grand Canyon look out for the king of the skies, the golden eagle.

5 Tortoises

Two species of desert tortoise, the Mojave and the Sonoran, are found in southern Utah, and in parts of Nevada and Arizona. These elusive creatures spend most of their lives underground.

6 Lizards

In Zion, eastern fence lizards are among 13 local species, while chuckwallas, short-horned, and collared lizards all inhabit the Grand Canyon and Death Valley. Most common in Death Valley is the banded lizard.

7 Bears

Black bears are occasionally seen on the higher plateaus at Zion, but both they and grizzlies have long since disappeared from the Grand Canyon area, and no bears live in the mountains surrounding Death Valley or the Grand Canyon.

8 Deer

The unmistakable stiff-legged jump and large ears of the mule deer distinguish it through your binoculars from its graceful relative, the white-tailed deer.

9 Snakes

Most species in the parks are harmless, but give rattlesnakes such as sidewinders a wide berth.

10 Mountain Lions

These shy creatures roam the Grand Canyon, Zion, and the mountains around Death Valley. They generally eat larger mammals such as mule deer and bighorn sheep.

One of Death Valley's mountain lions

Natural Formations

1 Atlatl Rock, Valley of Fire
MAP U2
The most famous petroglyph carved into this rock depicts an atlatl, a notched stick used to add speed and distance to a thrown spear.

2 Funeral Mountains, Death Valley
MAP S1
A geological fault line was responsible for tilting these spectacular mountains on their sides.

3 Temple of Sinawava, Zion National Park
MAP V1
The temple is, in fact, an awe-inspiring mass of red rock. The religious name echoes many others in the park.

4 Great White Throne, Zion National Park
MAP V1
The sheer face of the Great White Throne, familiar to climbers worldwide, rises a staggering 2,200 ft (670 m) from the canyon floor, making it one of the tallest monoliths in the world.

5 Kolob Arch, Zion National Park
MAP V1
Kolob Arch is too inaccessible to permit accurate measurements of its bulk, but it is thought to be as much as 230 ft (70 m) high and 310 ft (95 m) wide.

6 Marble Canyon, Grand Canyon
MAP V2
The towering limestone walls of this canyon gave the upper section of the Grand Canyon its name.

Elephant Rock in the Valley of Fire State Park

7 Elephant Rock, Valley of Fire
MAP U2
Accessible via a short trail from the eastern entrance, this strange sandstone formation resembles the head of an elephant – albeit with an oversize trunk.

8 Inner Gorge, Grand Canyon
MAP V2
Sheer granite cliffs drop 1,000 ft (300 m) to the canyon floor to form this vertiginous gorge. Two nerve-testing suspension bridges make the crossing near Phantom Ranch.

9 San Francisco Mountains, Grand Canyon
MAP V2
Named the "Kingdom of St. Francis" by explorer Marcos de Niza, the range rises to an impressive height of 12,655 ft (3,857 m), the highest point in the state of Arizona.

10 Panamint Mountains, Death Valley
MAP S2
The Panamint Mountains are one of five mountain ranges in Death Valley. Head for Aguereberry Point to take in amazing views of the Funeral Mountains and the Sierra Nevada beyond.

See map on p110–11

Places to Eat

El Tovar Dining Room

1 El Tovar Dining Room, Grand Canyon

MAP V2 ▪ El Tovar Hotel, South Rim ▪ 928 638 2631 ▪ $$

Built of pine logs and stone, and featuring fine china and crystal. Fresh seafood is flown in daily, and the veal dishes are excellent.

2 Coronado Room, Grand Canyon

MAP V2 ▪ Best Western Squire Inn, Tusayan ▪ 928 638 2681 ▪ $$

Prime rib, chicken marsala, and stuffed trout are favorites at this Spanish-style eatery.

3 Bright Angel Lodge Restaurant, Grand Canyon

MAP V2 ▪ Bright Angel Lodge ▪ 928 638 2631 ▪ $

This is the place to come for hearty Southwest American fare.

4 Arizona Room, Grand Canyon

MAP V2 ▪ Bright Angel Lodge ▪ 928 638 2631 ▪ $$

A Southwest decor in muted pastels is the setting for the all-American favorite of big steaks, baked potatoes, and crisp salads.

5 Stovepipe Wells Village, Death Valley

MAP S2 ▪ Stovepipe Wells ▪ 760 786 2387 ▪ $

The Toll Road Restaurant offers eclectic fare all year long.

6 The Spotted Dog Café, Zion

MAP U1 ▪ Springdale ▪ 435 772 3244 ▪ Open for dinner only (also breakfast Mar–Nov) ▪ $$

Among the house specialties are salads, pasta, red trout, chicken, Utah lamb, and Black Angus beef.

7 Picnic Areas, Zion Canyon and Springdale

MAP U1 ▪

Buy provisions at Oscar's Café and a bumbleberry pie at the Bumbleberry Restaurant for an alfresco meal in a nearby picnic area.

8 East Zion Thunderbird Lodge Restaurant, Mt. Carmel

MAP U1 ▪ Mt. Carmel Jtn ▪ 435 648 2203 ▪ $

American fare in a family dining room, where the pies, breads, and sweet rolls are all home-made.

9 The Inn at Furnace Creek Dining Room, Death Valley

MAP S1 ▪ Furnace Creek Inn ▪ 760 786 2345 ▪ Open mid-Oct to mid-May ▪ $$$

Elegant dining room with lace table-cloths, firelight flickering on adobe walls, and views of the Panamint Mountains. Continental fare is served from a varied à la carte menu.

10 Maswik Lodge Cafeteria, Grand Canyon

MAP V2 ▪ Maswik Lodge ▪ 303 297 2757 ▪ $

Wholesome food at reasonable prices. For a pre- or post-meal drink the lodge includes a sports bar with a wide-screen TV.

Places to Stay

(1) Bright Angel Lodge, Grand Canyon

MAP V2 ▪ South Rim ▪ 928 638 2631
▪ www.grandcanyonlodges.com ▪ $$
This lovely timber lodge consists of a rambling old building plus several private cabins, some right by the rim.

(2) El Tovar Hotel, Grand Canyon

MAP V2 ▪ South Rim ▪ 928 638 2631
▪ www.grand canyonlodges.com
▪ $$
Historic hotel built by pioneer resort builders, the Fred Harvey Company, in 1905. It is patterned after the great hunting lodges of Europe with a stone fireplace and mounted animals.

(3) Grand Canyon Lodge

MAP V2 ▪ Bright Angel Point
▪ 303 297 2757 ▪ www.grandcanyon lodgenorth.com ▪ $$
The only hotel accommodation on the North Rim of the canyon, this lodge comprises cabins and a few modern motel rooms. Advance reservations are essential.

(4) Furnace Creek Inn, Death Valley

MAP S1 ▪ Furnace Creek ▪ 760 786 2345 ▪ Open mid-October to mid-May ▪ $$$
Elegant and expensive, with glorious views of the Panamint Mountains. Guest rooms have quality furnishings.

Furnace Creek Inn, Death Valley

PRICE CATEGORIES
For a standard, double room per night (with breakfast if included), taxes, and extra charges.

$ under $100 $$$100–200 $$$ over $200

(5) Zion Lodge

MAP U1 ▪ Zion National Park
▪ 435 772 7700 ▪ $$
The complex includes 40 cabins with gas log fireplaces, baths, and private porches, and 80 rooms, most with two queen-size beds.

(6) Best Western Zion Park Inn

MAP U1 ▪ 1215 Zion Park Blvd, Springdale ▪ 435 772 3200 ▪ $$
At the foot of The Watchman, the 120 rooms here are climate-controlled and some have kitchenettes.

(7) Desert Pearl Inn, Zion

MAP U1 ▪ 707 Zion Park Blvd, Springdale ▪ 435 772 8888 ▪ $$
Modern hotel by the Virgin River with great views, huge rooms, and a pool.

(8) Camper Village

MAP V2 ▪ Tusayan ▪ 928 638 2887 ▪ $
With 250 RV hook-ups and 100 tent sites, this is one of the larger, privately run, year-round campgrounds.

(9) Furnace Creek Ranch, Death Valley

MAP S1 ▪ Furnace Creek ▪ 760 786 2361 ▪ $$
The rustic hostelry offers two spring-fed pools (the water is very warm), golf, tennis, and horseback riding.

(10) Phantom Ranch, Grand Canyon

MAP V2 ▪ Colorado River ▪ 303 297 2757 ▪ www.grandcanyonlodges.com
▪ $
The only ranch at the bottom of the Grand Canyon. Only accessible to hikers, who share dorms, and mule riders, who can reserve cabins.

See map on pp110–11

Hiking Trails

1 Mouse's Tank, Valley of Fire

"Mouse" was the name of a Native American outlaw. The moderately easy trail to Mouse's Tank (a series of natural catchments) passes the best petroglyphs in the park.

2 Canyon Overlook Trail, Zion National Park

This moderate, short day-hike to the overlook provides great views of lower Zion Canyon.

3 Observation Point Trail, Zion

The 8-mile (12.9-km) round-trip hike is moderately difficult to Hidden Canyon, then strenuous to Observation Point. There is a 2,148-ft (655-m) elevation gain.

4 Riverside Walk, Zion

This paved walk at the base of a gorge is especially delightful in early November when the fall foliage is at its most beautiful.

5 Bright Angel Trail, Grand Canyon

This popular 9.2-mile (14.8-km) trail drops 4,400 ft (1,342 m) to the Colorado River. You'll need two days – and a backcountry permit – to get to the river and back, so most visitors use the trail for shorter one-day hikes instead.

6 Rim Trail, Grand Canyon

Extending from the Village area, the partially paved trail can be accessed at many points along Hermit Road and its terminus at the South Kaibab trailhead. There is little elevation change and great views.

7 South Kaibab Trail, Grand Canyon

Access to the trailhead is by shuttle bus. The steep trail descends 4,500 ft (1,372 m), with no water along the down-and-back 14-mile (22.5-km) route.

8 Wildrose Canyon to Wildrose Peak, Death Valley

A 4-mile (6-km) climb through woodland to the crest of the Panamint Mountains. Superb views.

9 Golden Canyon to Zabriskie Point, Death Valley

A low-elevation, 6-mile (9.6-km) round-trip hike, traversing an area of fully exposed rock strata that represents millions of years.

10 Coffin Peak Trail, Death Valley

This easy trail starts at Dante's View, following a canyon into the Black Mountains. Vegetation is dominated by spiny desert shrubs.

A view along the Bright Angel Trail, Grand Canyon

Commercial Tours

1 GC Flight
702 629 7776
■ www.gcflight.com

This company runs helicopter and airplane flights, as well as motor-coach tours, from Las Vegas to the Grand Canyon and Hoover Dam. Flights can also be taken over the Strip.

2 Maverick Helicopters
702 261 0007 ■ www.maverickhelicopter.com

The Wind Dancer Air and Landing Tour includes landing on the floor of the Grand Canyon, a champagne picnic, and views of Lake Mead, Hoover Dam, and an extinct volcano.

3 Awesome Adventures
800 519 2243 ■ www.awesomeadventures.com

Several options for areas to tour include the desert, Lake Mead, and the Valley of Fire. Some tours include lunch and hotel pick-up.

4 Grand Canyon Express
800 843 8724
■ www.airvegas.com

Grand Canyon Express offers standard air, boat, and motor-coach tours as well as VIP options.

5 Zion Rock and Mountain Guides
435 772 3303
■ www.zionrockguides.com

These expert guides and outfitters are specialists in kitting out hikers for the canyoneering day-hike through Zion Narrows, in addition to offering daily hiker shuttles and climbing excursions.

6 Zion Canyon Field Institute
435 772 3264 ■ www.zionpark.org

This institute runs inexpensive talks, walks, and expeditions in Zion National Park, covering a broad range of topics, such as history, wildlife, photography, and geology.

Pink Jeep Tour in the desert

7 Pink Jeep Tours
888 900 4480
■ www.pinkjeeptours.com

Known for its knowledgeable guides, Pink Jeep offers several half- and full-day tours in the area. Tours are conducted in 10-person vehicles, so groups are kept to a manageable size. It is also one of the few tour companies with off-road permits.

8 Canyon Explorations
928 774 4559 ■ www.canyonexplorations.com

One of several companies providing hiking, interpretive trips, and white-water rafting in the Grand Canyon.

9 ATV Wilderness Tours
888 656 2887 ■ www.atvadventures.com

Year-round guided trips in four-wheel all-terrain vehicles and Jeeps. Three- to six-hour outings are available. The company is based in Hurricane, near St. George, Utah.

10 Adventure Photo Tours
888 363 8687 ■ www.adventurephototours.com

Full- and half-day tours hit the highlights so visitors have the chance to capture ghost towns, wild horses, petroglyphs, old mines, sandstone formations, and wildflowers on camera.

See map on pp110–11 ←

Streetsmart

Fremont Street Experience

Getting To and Around Las Vegas

Arriving by Air

All international and domestic flights to and from Las Vegas use **McCarran International Airport**. Although the runways are close to the southern end of the Strip, it is 3 miles (5 km) by road from the terminals to the nearest part of the Strip, and 7 miles (11 km) to Downtown. Allow at least 10 minutes to travel between the airport and hotels on the Strip; in rush-hour traffic (weekdays 7–9am and 4–7pm) the trip can be very slow.

As the Las Vegas Monorail does not serve the airport, the easiest way to reach your accommodation is by taxi, which will cost anything from $16 to the southern end of the Strip to $40 for Downtown. Rates depend on the driving time, so if you're in rush-hour traffic it can be expensive.

It is also possible to ride in a shared **Bell Limousine** shuttle bus, which takes passengers on request to specific hotels. However, if your hotel is low on the list it can take an hour or more.

Direct buses do not connect the airport with the Strip and Downtown. Instead, catch RTC bus 109 to the South Strip Transfer Terminal, and change there onto the Strip & Downtown Express service.

It is only really worth renting a car if you plan to travel beyond the city. In any case, renting from the airport is not a quick process, as you can only pick up cars from the McCarran Rent-A-Car Center, 3 miles (5 km) southwest of the airport, which is reached using the free shuttle buses that stop outside both terminals.

Arriving by Bus

There are no train services to Las Vegas. Long-distance buses, operated by **Greyhound**, do however run to the city from Los Angeles (taking between 5 and 7 hours) and Salt Lake City (taking around 8 hours), both of which are served by Amtrak trains, and from Phoenix, which is not. Las Vegas's Greyhound station is Downtown, beside the Plaza hotel.

Arriving by Road

The main – and busiest – driving route to and from Las Vegas is the I-15 interstate, which connects the city with Salt Lake City in Utah, 420 miles (676 km) northeast, and Los Angeles in California, 270 miles (435 km) southwest. On Friday evenings in particular, the road is usually crammed with visitors heading up from LA for the weekend. It is best to stay on the interstate until you're as close as possible to your hotel; driving on the Strip is generally much slower.

Arriving from the east or Arizona, you're most likely to approach Las Vegas along US-93, which crosses into Nevada over the Hoover Dam. This road runs straight to Downtown; turn off west to get to the Strip.

Getting Around by Bus

Las Vegas's **Regional Transportation Commission (RTC)** runs a comprehensive network of buses throughout the city. Most visitors, however, use its two principal routes, the Deuce and the Strip & Downtown Express (SDX), both of which are wheelchair accessible.

The Deuce runs 24 hours daily along the entire Strip, from Mandalay Bay to the Stratosphere, stopping outside every major casino, and also continues north into and around Downtown.

The Strip & Downtown Express (9am–midnight daily) starts at the South Strip Transfer Terminal (SSTT), 3 miles (5 km) south of Mandalay Bay, which is served by separate buses to and from the airport. The SDX runs north along the Strip, stopping opposite Mandalay Bay, and outside the MGM Grand, Paris, and Wynn; it then heads, via the Convention Center and Fremont Street Downtown, to the Las Vegas Premium Outlets (North) shopping center. On its return journey south, back along the Strip, it stops outside the Fashion Show Mall, Bellagio, Excalibur, and Mandalay Bay.

Before you board any bus, you have to buy a ticket from the machines located next to each stop. A 2-hour pass costs $6, a 24-hour pass $8, and a 3-day pass $20.

Getting Around by Car

Although cruising along the Strip can be a real thrill, driving is not a quick or convenient way to get from casino to casino. A car is essential, on the other hand, if you plan to explore the outlying neighborhoods, or to venture anywhere beyond the city. Nearly all of the Strip hotel and casinos charge for parking in high-rise garages at the back (often a long walk from the property itself), as well as more expensive valet parking. Downtown, parking is generally more restricted; most Fremont Street hotels require joining their rewards program for free parking.

All car-rental chains that were formerly based at the airport now operate from the McCarran Rent-A-Car Center, just off the Strip 3 miles (5 km) south of Mandalay Bay, and the same distance southwest of the airport, to which it's connected by frequent free shuttles. Renting a compact car here typically costs from around $35 per day, or $150 per week. Although you can also rent a car at all the major hotels, you'll almost certainly pay much higher rates if you do. Overseas visitors need a full driving license from their own countries; an International Driving License is not sufficient. Rental companies will not rent cars to under-21s, while under-25s can expect to pay a premium.

Getting Around by Monorail

The **Las Vegas Monorail** runs parallel to the Strip on its eastern side, from the MGM Grand to the SLS hotel via the Convention Center (7am–midnight Mon, 7am–2am Tue–Thu, 7am–3am Fri–Sun). It does not serve the airport or Downtown. As the stations are a long way back from the Strip, it is only useful for longer journeys. A one-ride ticket costs $5, a one-day pass $12, and a three-day pass $28. In addition, three free smaller-scale tram systems link some of the casinos on the west side of the Strip. One connects Excalibur with Luxor and Mandalay Bay; another runs from Bellagio to the Monte Carlo, via Aria and the Crystals mall; and the last travels between TI and the Mirage.

Getting Around by Taxi

Hotel entrances on the Strip and Downtown are the best places to find cabs; you can't simply hail a passing taxi. The standard fare includes an initial fee of $3.50, plus $2.88 for each additional mile, and about 50 cents a minute when stopped at a red light or stalled in traffic. In heavy traffic, it can cost more than $20 to go from one end of the Strip to the other.

Getting Around on Foot

You may be surprised by quite how much you walk in Las Vegas; it can take upwards of ten minutes to walk from one casino to its next-door neighbor, while the entire Strip stretches for 4 miles (6 km). Casinos are well connected, sidewalks are wide, and the terrain is flat, but in summer the heat can be merciless so be sure to drink plenty of water. Distances are too great, however, to walk anywhere beyond the Strip itself or within the small Downtown area.

Practical Information

Passports and Visas

Citizens from Australia, New Zealand, Japan, Germany, France, the UK, and many other European countries can visit the US for up to 90 days without a visa, so long as they have a valid passport. Before you travel from your home country, however, you must apply for the Visa Waiver Program online, via **ESTA** (Electronic System for Travel Authorization) and pay a fee of $14. Registration remains valid for two years. Note that to use ESTA, your passport must be machine-readable; if you have an older, non-readable passport, either get a new one before you travel, or apply for a visa. Children must carry their own personal passports. Canadian visitors simply need to show their passports to enter the US.

Visitors from countries for which visas are required must apply to a US consulate or embassy in their country, and may be asked for evidence of financial solvency and proof that they intend to return home – usually a return plane ticket.

Customs Regulations and Immigration

International travelers who have the necessary ESTA authorization or visa pass through immigration control at their point of arrival on US soil. If you are not on a direct flight to Las Vegas you will need to go through the procedure at your first port of entry. Just fill in the green form distributed on incoming flights.

Adult non-residents can bring in a limited number of duty-free goods, including 0.2 gallons (1 liter) of alcohol, 200 cigarettes, 100 cigars (including Cuban), and up to $100 worth of gifts. Cash amounts over $10,000 must be declared.

Travel Safety Advice

Visitors can get up-to-date travel safety information from the **Foreign and Commonwealth Office** in the UK, the **State Department** in the US, and the **Department of Foreign Affairs and Trade** in Australia.

Travel Insurance

While not compulsory for visitors to the US, travel insurance is emphatically recommended: emergency medical and dental care can be extremely expensive. In most cases, people incurring medical expenses are required to pay before leaving the clinic.

Health

Visitors to Las Vegas do not require any vaccinations. The main health issue for most visitors is exposure to the desert sun. Use high-factor sun creams, especially when using the hotel pool, and drink plenty of fluids.

In a medical emergency, call 911 immediately. Both the **Sunrise Hospital** and the **University Medical Center** have 24-hour emergency rooms. Pharmacies on the Strip include the 24-hour **CVS** pharmacy beside the Monte Carlo, and **Walgreens** beside The Palazzo.

Beware of rattlesnakes and scorpions. Before you go, learn how to treat their bites (getting medical help as quickly as possible is recommended). Other dangerous desert animals and insects are mountain lions, bears, wild boar, killer bees, and centipedes. Wildlife may seem tame but will attack if they feel threatened.

Personal Security

Las Vegas's casinos are safe places to be; there is too much security in place for you to be in danger of crime. Elsewhere in the city, take all the usual precautions; keep cash and valuables well hidden. Don't tell anyone your hotel room number, and be vigilant in multi-story parking garages.

Currency and Banking

The US dollar is divided into 100 cents (called pennies). Coins come in one cent, five cent (nickel), ten cent (dime), 25 cent (quarter), and 50 cent denominations. If you are unfamiliar with US banknotes, be warned that they are notoriously hard to differentiate between; take care when handing over cash to taxi

...rivers and shop keepers. A $1 "bill" is the same size and color as a $20. Denominations start at $1 and run as high as $100.

You'll be expected to use a credit or debit card to pay for all significant transactions in Las Vegas. Even if you have paid your hotel bill in advance, you'll also have to leave a credit card imprint when you check in to cover any further incidental expenses. All major credit cards are accepted everywhere. If you are traveling from overseas, check what extra fees your bank may charge for transactions in the US, and if necessary, consider obtaining a card that charges no such fees.

It is not a good idea to bring foreign cash, or traveler's checks issued in foreign currencies, to Las Vegas. Banks are few and far between, and especially rare on the Strip, and while cashiers' offices in all the casinos will exchange foreign money, they charge punitive rates. Expect instead to obtain any cash you need from ATMs, which are found in all the casinos and many other public places. Almost all ATMs in the city, however, charge a fee for each cash withdrawal, typically $3, so it's worth taking out larger amounts each time you do so.

Traveler's checks issued in US dollars are accepted like cash everywhere, but few visitors use them these days.

Most hotels will cash the personal checks of guests – but not non-guests – who have US bank accounts.

Opening Hours

Shops and attractions on the Strip and Downtown tend to be geared towards the needs of visitors, opening every day of the week at 9am or 10am and remaining open well into the evening, especially on weekends. Las Vegas banks open from 9am until either 5 or 6pm Monday through Friday, and 9am–1pm on Saturday, but there are very few on or near the Strip. Branches located in supermarkets tend to have longer hours and stay open all day on Saturday and sometimes on Sunday afternoon.

Casinos are open all day, as are some restaurants and bars, and can be busy at both 3am and 3pm. The lack of windows and clocks on gaming floors can make it hard to judge the passing of time.

Time Difference

Las Vegas operates on Pacific Standard Time, which is the same as California, 3 hours behind Eastern Standard Time, and 8 hours behind Greenwich Mean Time. Clocks move 1 hour forward on the second Sunday in March, and 1 hour back on the first Sunday in November.

Electrical Appliances

As throughout the US, the electrical current in Las Vegas is 110 volts and 60 hertz. Visitors from abroad will need a Type A or Type B adaptor plug to use the two-prong sockets, and may also need a voltage converter to operate their own appliances. Most charging leads for foreign phones and laptops incorporate voltage converters that will work in the US.

DIRECTORY

PASSPORTS AND VISAS

ESTA
🌐 esta.cbp.dhs.gov

CONSULATES

Australian Consulate
Century Plaza Tower, LA
📞 310 229 2327

British Consulate
2029 Century Park E., LA
📞 310 789 0031

Canadian Consulate
550 S. Hope St, LA
📞 213 346 2700

New Zealand Consulate
2425 Olympic Blvd, Santa Monica
📞 310 566 6555

TRAVEL SAFETY ADVICE

Australia
🌐 smartraveller.gov.au

United Kingdom
🌐 gov.uk/foreign-travel-advice

United States
🌐 travel.state.gov

HEALTH

CVS
MAP Q2 ▪ 3758 S. Las Vegas Blvd
📞 702 262 9028

Sunrise Hospital
MAP N5 ▪ 3186 S. Maryland Pkwy
📞 702 731 8000

University Medical Center
MAP K2 ▪ 1800 W. Charleston Blvd
📞 702 383 2000

Walgreens
MAP P2 ▪ 3339 S. Las Vegas Blvd
📞 702 369 8166

Communications

All Las Vegas hotels offer in-room Wi-Fi. It is not exactly free – it's one of the main elements of the so-called "resort fees" charged by most hotels. Be warned that the fee may only cover one device; a couple traveling with a smartphone and a laptop each may have to pay four times over. Many casino-hotels offer free Wi-Fi in their public areas. You can also get free Wi-Fi at the airport, in coffee bars like Starbucks and Coffee Bean & Tea Leaf, and in Apple stores.

Make sure you're aware what your hotel charges for phone calls. Many include free local calls as part of the resort fee, and a few even offer free long-distance calls. Others charge $1 for a short local call or toll-free number, and exorbitant rates for anything more.

Public payphones are now almost nonexistent. Hotels, tour operators, and other businesses can be contacted via toll-free numbers, which start with 800, 844, 855, 866, 877, or 888.

Any cellphone will almost certainly work in Las Vegas. Travelers from overseas, however, should make sure they know what their phone provider charges for calls, texts, and using data to go online. Roaming charges can be enormous. Foreign visitors are advised to go online using hotel Wi-Fi.

The cheapest way to make long-distance calls is to use an application like Skype. Gas stations, convenience stores, and hotel gift shops sell prepaid phone cards, which you can also use to make cut-rate calls.

To place a call within Las Vegas, you must dial the 702 area code. When calling outside the area, dial 1 followed by the area code and seven-digit number. For international calls, dial 011, then the country code, then the number, omitting the initial 0.

You can have mail sent either to your hotel or to "General Delivery" at any Post Office in the city.

Weather

Las Vegas is a desert city, receiving an average of just 4 inches (10 cm) of rainfall per year. The summer is excruciatingly hot, with average daily highs in July and August of well over 100 °F (38 °C). Winter is less predictable; the nights can drop below freezing in December and January, but conditions may be surprisingly balmy during the day. The best seasons to visit are spring and fall.

The weather can present a variety of dangerous situations, especially in the canyons, where sudden summer storms can cause flash floods. Don't try to drive through flooded areas. If water begins to rise over the road, it is actually best to abandon your car and move to high ground.

If you are going for a hike, always notify someone of your route and when you expect to return. Never venture into the desert alone, and don't go hiking without a map and a good compass, even if you have a GPS.

The dry heat of the summers can often be underestimated by visitors, and hikers especially are advised to carry at least a gallon (4 liters) of drinking water per person for each day of walking. Carry water for your car engine, too. It is also extremely important for visitors to guard against the risk of forest fires, which can affect the area with devastating results.

At higher elevations the sun can be surprisingly strong, even on cloudy days. If planning on hiking or engaging in other outdoor activities during the summer, a sun hat should be worn to prevent heatstroke. Even if you spend only minutes outside, you should protect your skin with sunscreen.

Visitor Information

The **Las Vegas Convention and Visitors Authority (LVCVA)** has an excellent website with details of accommodation, attractions, and shopping, but it's not worth making the effort to visit the **Las Vegas Visitor Center**, adjoining the Convention Center on Paradise Road (open 8am–5:30pm Mon–Fri).

If you are driving to Las Vegas, however, do stop along the way to pick up information and discount coupons when you enter the state at the well-stocked **Nevada Welcome Centers** (open 8am– 4:30pm Mon–Fri), in Mesquite as you app-roach from Utah, in

Laughlin at Casino Drive, and near Boulder City en route when driving from Arizona.

The city's main newspapers, the *Las Vegas Review-Journal* and the *Las Vegas Sun*, are sold together, while each runs its own website, packed with news, reviews, and listings. The Friday edition is best for entertainment listings and the latest restaurant reviews.

Other sources of information include free magazines *Vegas Seven* and *Las Vegas Weekly*, both with online editions. There are many other free monthly and weekly magazines distributed in the city – you'll almost certainly find one in your hotel room.

Travelers with Specific Needs

Las Vegas caters well to travelers with disabilities; provisions are summarized on the "Travelers with Special Needs" page of the LVCVA website.

The airport is easily accessible, while every taxi firm has lift-equipped vans. Both **Bell Limousine** shuttle buses and RTC city buses are also wheelchair accessible.

All casino-hotels provide wheelchair access, and offer rooms with roll-in or transfer showers. Many also offer facilities for gamblers with disabilities, including braille bingo for blind players.

All car-rental chains offer adapted vehicles, and the **Nevada**

Department of Motor Vehicles will issue visitors free, short-term disabled parking permits. Mobility equipment can be rented from the **Ability Center**.

Trips and Tours

Neither walking tours nor bus tours are popular in Las Vegas. It takes too long to walk from one casino to the next, and you can't see them properly from a passing bus. **Gray Line** offer bus tours farther afield, including to the Hoover Dam and Grand Canyon National Park.

"Flightseeing" tours are popular, ranging from 15-minute flights over the Strip to trips to the Grand Canyon.

DIRECTORY

VISITOR INFORMATION

Las Vegas Review-Journal
W reviewjournal.com

Las Vegas Sun
W lasvegassun.com

Las Vegas Visitor Center
MAP N3 ■ 3150 Paradise Rd
C 877 847 4858
W lasvegas.com

Las Vegas Weekly
W lasvegasweekly.com

Vegas Seven
W vegasseven.com

Nevada Welcome Centers
US-93 Boulder City
406 N. Sandhill Blvd, Mesquite
1555 Casino Dr., Laughlin

Useful websites
W cheapovegas.com
W downtown.vegas
W eatinglv.com

W gayvegas.com
W lasvegasadvisor.com
W lvol.com
W ratevegas.com
W travelnevada.com
W vegas.com
W vitalvegas.com

TRAVELERS WITH SPECIFIC NEEDS

Ability Center
MAP B5 ■ 6001 S. Decatur Blvd
C 702 434 3030
W abilitycenter.com

Bell Limousine
C 702 739 7990
W belllimousine.com

Las Vegas Convention and Visitors Authority
W lasvegas.com

Nevada Department of Motor Vehicles
C 702 486 4368
W dmvnv.com

RTC
W catride.com

TRIPS AND TOURS

GC Flight
C 702 629 7776
W gcflight.com

Grand Canyon Airlines
C 702 835 8484
W grandcanyon airlines.com

Gray Line
C 702 739 7777
W grayline.com

Maverick Helicopters
C 702 261 0007
W maverickhelicopter.com

Scenic Airlines
C 702 638 3300
W scenic.com

Sundance Helicopters
C 702 736 0606
W sundance helicopters.com

Dining Tips

Gone are the days when you could only eat cheaply and badly in Las Vegas. The city now holds some of the finest restaurants in the US, thanks largely to chefs with renowned high-end restaurants elsewhere who have been offered irresistible sums to open outlets in Las Vegas's casinos. Book well in advance if you have your heart set on eating at a specific restaurant. Staying in a casino does not give you priority booking in its restaurants.

Fine dining does not come cheap – it's not unusual to pay more than $100 for a meal – but the food scene has become a major reason to visit. In addition, every casino offers a variety of cheaper options, usually including a round-the-clock "coffee shop" serving diner food, and also an all-you-can-eat buffet. The most upscale casinos offer "gourmet buffets" where dinner costs as much as $55, but you can still get a decent buffet meal elsewhere for under $20.

Shopping Tips

Shopping is also a prime attraction here. The Strip has some of the fanciest malls in the country, including The Forum Shops at Caesars Palace (see pp20–21) and The Venetian's Grand Canal Shoppes (see p17). You can also shop well away from the casinos, for example in the Fashion Show Mall on the Strip (see p72), or at the Premium Outlet malls.

Visitors should not expect much shopping in Downtown, which has almost no shops.

Where to Stay

Deciding where you stay while you're in Las Vegas will have a major impact on your vacation. Many first-time visitors, wary of the city's round-the-clock, all-action image, opt for a hotel that's neither on the Strip nor Downtown for a quieter experience.

On the whole, Las Vegas is something of an all-or-nothing destination; if the prospect of spending your time in huge casino-hotels, in a hyped-up and heavily commercialized atmosphere, doesn't appeal to you, then perhaps Las Vegas simply isn't the right destination for you in the first place.

The Strip consists almost exclusively of massive casinos that are also hotels – so much so that more than half of the world's 40 largest hotels are concentrated along its 4-mile (6-km) stretch. In addition to an extensive gambling area (usually at street level), each holds a number of restaurants, bars, shops, nightclubs, and one or more theater-sized showrooms. Most are also architectural landmarks in their own right, built to resemble anything from a major European city to an ancient Egyptian pyramid, and adorned with spectacular attractions like the Fountains of Bellagio (see p81) or the Eiffel Tower at Paris (see p43). If you do any sightseeing in Las Vegas, most of the sights you see will be the casinos.

Even if you're not interested in gambling, it makes sense to stay in one of the hotels that make Las Vegas what it is. Their many thousands of guest rooms are invariably located in high-rise towers that soar above the casino itself, and thus well removed from the frenzy below. There's always the risk of having noisy neighbors who lurch back to their rooms at 3am, though, so if peace is a priority it's worth choosing a hotel that doesn't have a reputation for nightlife and partying. Typical rooms tend to resemble what you would find in an upscale hotel elsewhere – they are seldom themed like the casinos – while those in properties like The Venetian (see pp16–17), Bellagio (see pp14–15), and Wynn (see pp18–19) are luxurious suites. Staying in such enormous hotels does of course have its downsides. You may well have to wait half an hour or more to check in when you first arrive, while in a property like The Venetian it can take twenty minutes to walk from your room to the Strip sidewalk.

There are strong arguments in favor of staying Downtown rather than the Strip. Apart from the Golden Nugget (see p39), the Downtown options are much more manageable in scale, and generally somewhat cheaper. Downtown conforms more to the old-fashioned, down-and-dirty image of Las Vegas as an edgy and hard-bitten Sin City, but also has more of a neighborhood feel.

Countless ordinary chain hotels and motels line the streets within a mile or two of the Strip, while outlying casino-hotels are found around the rest of the city. It is really only practical to stay in those areas if you have a car. It can be unpleasant to walk even half a mile between your hotel and the Strip, along the traffic-choked streets in the desert heat.

Room Rates and Booking

The most important thing you need to know about accommodation rates in Las Vegas is that every room in every hotel changes in price every night. A room that costs $49 on a Monday or Tuesday can easily cost $199 that same Friday or Saturday. The one sure-fire way to save money is to time your visit for weekdays rather than weekends. It may be worth considering changing to a cheaper hotel for the weekend; maybe stay on the Strip during the week and move Downtown for the weekend.

Other factors that affect room rates on specific days include major concerts and events – even sports events elsewhere, which nonetheless attract gamblers to Las Vegas – and something that's far less obvious to vacationers: whether there's a major convention in town. During the three largest annual conventions – the Consumer Electronics Show (CES) in January, the National Association of Broadcasters in April, and the Specialty Equipment Manufacturers'

Association in November – well over 100,000 delegates flood into town. Do your utmost not to coincide with them: not only will hotel rates be at their highest, but traffic is heavy, and the lines for restaurants, bars, and shows can be daunting.

If you are booking your own accommodation, you will find the cheapest rates on the websites of the casinos themselves, as listed in this book. Comparison shopping is easy: there is a hotel booking facility on the official **Las Vegas Convention and Visitors Authority** website. Also, most casinos belong to large corporations that own several properties. If you search on the Mandalay Bay website, for example, you will also be shown prices for a dozen or more other MGM Resorts hotels, from Excalibur *(see p43)* to Bellagio, while looking up Caesars Palace will also give you rates for Caesars Entertainment's entire portfolio. Once you have discovered the relevant rates, it can be worth phoning the hotel directly to talk with the reservations department. Discussing your needs with a person who knows the hotel intimately will help you get exactly the room to suit you.

Various discounts are available, often including a ten percent reduction for members of the **American Automobile Association** that also extends to corresponding international organizations, such as the British **AA**. The days are long gone, though, when

casual visitors could get free rooms for gambling in the casinos – these days, you would have to have a proven record of gambling thousands of dollars before they offer you a room.

You should make bookings well in advance, though last-minute bargains are always possible, on weekdays at least. Bear in mind that room rates quoted online won't include either the compulsory "resort fees" charged by almost all the casinos for facilities such as in-room Wi-Fi, which typically cost an additional $15–35 per night, or room taxes, which add up to 12 per cent.

Finally, one way you might find an appreciably better deal is if you book your accommodation as part of an overall package, including your flights to and from Las Vegas, and potentially car rental as well. All airlines that serve the city offer such packages, as do many general travel operators, and also the hotels themselves.

DIRECTORY

AA
📞 0800 316 2456 or 0191 503 1001
🌐 theaa.com

Accommodation Booking Websites
🌐 booking.com
🌐 expedia.com
🌐 priceline.com

American Automobile Association
📞 866 222 6595
🌐 aaa.com

Las Vegas Convention and Visitors Authority
🌐 lasvegas.com

Getting Married in Las Vegas

Las Vegas Weddings

Getting married continues to rank among the major reasons to come to Las Vegas – the bureaucracy is minimal, the costs are (or at least can be) comparatively low, and, of course, it is a great place to have a party. While the spontaneous ceremony in the dead of night may be a staple of Hollywood movies, most Las Vegas weddings are far from kitsch or frivolous, and the wedding industry is a multimillion-dollar business here.

All the major casinos have their own chapels and wedding-planning services, while countless private chapels are dotted around the city, and especially along the stretch of Las Vegas Boulevard that runs south from Downtown to the Strip proper. Almost all of them are capable of hosting hugely opulent and luxurious weddings if you are happy to pay the appropriate price; be warned, though, that at the cheaper end of the market they can be somewhat dispiriting and soulless places. In total, Las Vegas chapels celebrate around 100,000 weddings each year.

The two busiest periods are Valentine's Day and New Year's Eve, which besides being a romantic date offers the prosaic advantage for US couples of entitling them to submit a joint tax return for the preceding year. Couples planning their wedding around those times should obtain licenses well in advance, to avoid long lines at the **Clark County Marriage License Bureau**.

Laws and Licenses

The marriage-license requirements in Nevada have traditionally been less stringent than those in other US states. No blood tests are needed, and neither is it necessary, after the license has been issued, to wait a set period before getting married.

To obtain a marriage license, both partners must appear at the County Clerk's office in the Clark County Marriage License Bureau, four blocks south of Fremont Street in Downtown Las Vegas. Both must be aged over 18 and carrying picture ID. Anyone aged between 16 and 18 must either have a consenting parent present, or be able to produce a notarized document from a parent giving his or her consent. Acceptable forms of ID are listed on the bureau's website. US citizens must also provide their Social Security numbers, but do not have to show the actual Social Security card. Applicants who have been married before must provide details of when and where their divorces were finalized, or their previous partners died, but do not have to show copies of divorce decrees or death certificates.

The marriage license costs $77, payable in cash or traveler's checks; credit cards are not accepted. The process is much quicker if you have already completed the application form online, using the bureau's website, in which case you simply need to take your reference number to the office's "express window."

Wedding Ceremonies

Nevada law requires that couples be married by civil marriage commissioners, justices of the peace, or bona fide ministers. The fastest and least expensive way to get married is to walk a single block from the Clark County Marriage License Bureau to the **Office of Civil Marriages**, where the commissioner will perform a civil ceremony for $75, payable by credit card. You can only do so, however, if you have made an appointment in advance, which is only possible via the Clark County website.

Be sure you go to the genuine Office of Civil Marriages; some wedding chapels deliberately give themselves very similar names to fool couples into paying for their ceremonies instead. In addition, touts wait outside hoping to lure couples away to nearby chapels.

Note too that a witness is required at all marriages. It is much better to bring someone you know to act as a witness, rather than use one of the assorted unsavory characters who are usually hanging around outside the office.

Costs and Options

The cheapest ceremony at a Las Vegas wedding chapel is liable to cost around $200. Expect to pay around $75 for the use of the chapel itself – or, in the case of the drive-through facility at **A Little White Wedding Chapel**, for the privilege of driving through their "Tunnel of Love" in your own vehicle – plus at least $50 for the minister, and more for any flowers and music.

Beyond those bare essentials, the possibilities are all but infinite. Obvious extras include limousine service, formal wedding gowns and tuxedos, and accessories such as garters and boutonniers. Then there are the only-in-Vegas options, such as hiring an Elvis impersonator – most chapels have one or more on tap, typically costing upwards of $200 – to walk the bride down the aisle, serenade the happy couple, or even perform the ceremony.

Pretty much whatever you can dream up for your wedding, Las Vegas will be happy to oblige. You can get married in the see-through underwater tunnel in Mandalay Bay's **Shark Reef Aquarium**; aboard a white wedding gondola on the Grand Canal in The Venetian (see pp16–17); or even beside the Colorado River at the bottom of the Grand Canyon, having flown there with **Sundance Helicopters**.

Gay and Lesbian Weddings

When same-sex marriage was declared legal in Nevada in 2014, obliging the Marriage License Bureau to start issuing licenses to same-sex couples, it triggered something of a gold rush for the city's in-casino and stand-alone wedding chapels. The wedding options for same-sex couples are limitless, and include some chapels dedicated specifically to gay and lesbian clients, including the **Gay Chapel of Las Vegas**.

Photography

The price of your wedding photos or video can form a major component of the overall cost of the ceremony. It is not unusual for a wedding chapel to forbid guests and participants from bringing their own cameras. Instead, you will have to use the chapel's own photographers, and pay for each individual print or copy.

DIRECTORY

LAWS AND LICENSES

Clark County Marriage License Bureau
MAP K4 ■ 201 E. Clark Ave
☎ 702 671 0600
ⓦ clarkcountynv.gov

Office of Civil Marriages
MAP K4 ■ 330 S. 3rd St
☎ 702 671 0577
ⓦ clarkcountynv.gov

WEDDING CHAPELS

Chapel of the Flowers
MAP L3 ■ 1717 Las Vegas Blvd S.
☎ 702 735 4331
ⓦ littlechapel.com

Gay Chapel of Las Vegas
MAP L4 ■ 1205 Las Vegas Blvd S.
☎ 702 384 0771
ⓦ gaychapeloflasvegas. com

Graceland Wedding Chapel
MAP K4 ■ 619 Las Vegas Blvd S.
☎ 702 382 0091
ⓦ gracelandchapel.com

Little Church of the West
MAP C5 ■ 4617 Las Vegas Blvd S.
☎ 702 739 7971
ⓦ littlechurchlv.com

A Little White Wedding Chapel
MAP L4 ■ 1301 Las Vegas Blvd S.
☎ 702 382 5943
ⓦ alittlewhitechapel.com

Mon Bel Ami Wedding Chapel
MAP K4 ■ 607 Las Vegas Blvd S.
☎ 702 388 4445
ⓦ monbelami.com

A Special Memory
MAP K4 ■ 800 South 4th St
☎ 702 384 2211
ⓦ aspecialmemory.com

Viva Las Vegas Wedding Chapels
MAP L4 ■ 1205 Las Vegas Blvd S.
☎ 702 384 0771
ⓦ vivalasvegas weddings.com

OTHER OPTIONS

Shark Reef Aquarium
MAP R1 ■ Mandalay Bay, 3950 Las Vegas Blvd S.
☎ 702 632 4555
ⓦ sharkreef.com

Sundance Helicopters
☎ 702 736 0606
ⓦ sundancehelicopters. com

Gambling in Las Vegas

The Basics

The essential point to remember about gambling in Las Vegas is that in almost every instance, no matter what the game, the casino has a built-in "edge" – the longer you play, the more likely the casino will end up with your money. That, after all, is the whole principle on which this preposterous (but endlessly exciting) city came to be built.

There are several very simple ways in which casinos make money from gamblers. First comes the intrinsic edge in the games themselves. This is at its most obvious in roulette, the game in which a successful bet on a number from 1 to 36 is paid off with 36 times your original stake, although in fact there are either 37 (on a single-zero table) or 38 (on the much more common double-zero table) possible outcomes.

On top of that, the rules of play are esentially rigged; because, for example, the dealer always has the last turn in blackjack, the casino can win without the dealer's hand ever having to be played.

Apart from those two points, the frenzied atmosphere of the casino floor is hardly a place to make financial decisions, particularly with alcohol flowing freely. Gamblers are always liable to play poorly and make mistakes. Thus several casinos are happy to provide gamblers with the so-called "basic strategy" in blackjack – a computer-generated system that sets out exactly what a player should do in any specific circumstance – because they know that almost no player has the will-power to stick to a boring, rigid system instead of following sudden "hunches."

To improve your chances of success, take regular breaks rather than gambling nonstop. Gambling can be a mentally and physically exhausting activity. If you spend more than an hour deciding whether to "hold 'em" or "fold 'em," or 2 hours hunched over a slot machine, fatigue could well set in.

And finally, just supposing you do get lucky, be sensible about how you react. Be careful not to boast about your winnings in any place where there is a chance strangers might hear you.

Rules and Etiquette

Gamblers at all table games use plastic chips as opposed to cash. You join a game by taking up a vacant seat and "buying in" – exchanging your cash with the dealer for the equivalent quantity of plastic chips.

There is a sign at every table announcing the "minimum bet" allowed for the current game. These minimum amounts vary from table to table, from casino to casino, and from neighborhood to neighborhood – so, minimum bets are typically lower in Downtown Las Vegas than they are on the Strip, lower at casinos like Circus Circus (see p81) than at Bellagio (see pp14–15), and lower in the public areas of Bellagio than in its roped-off high-rollers' rooms. The minimum bets also vary according to the time of day; you will find they are much lower at 11am on a Monday morning than they are at midnight on a Saturday. Always ensure you know the current minimum bet, and understand how it works for the game. For example, if there is a $10 minimum bet at roulette, you can make ten separate bets of $1 per spin, while a $10 minimum on blackjack obliges you to stake at least $10 per hand, no matter how many hands you are playing.

While the casinos of Las Vegas are relaxed in terms of how gamblers are dressed, and they are more than happy to ply them with drinks, visitors are nonetheless expected to behave appropriately. Try to touch your cards as little as possible when playing blackjack, for example, and in all games you should not attempt to touch or move your stake once play is underway. Note that on table games, it is customary to tip the dealer following a sizable win.

Underage Gambling

It is illegal in the state of Nevada for anyone under the age of 21 to gamble. Minors who are caught gambling are either arrested or given a citation, and could potentially face six months in jail. What is more, if you win a jackpot and you are not carrying the ID to prove that you are in fact over 21, you will not even be allowed to keep your winnings.

Slot Clubs and Players Clubs

Anyone who comes to Las Vegas intending to spend any significant length of time gambling should sign up for the "slot club" or "players club." These clubs exists in each and every casino. Membership of these clubs is free, and it enables you to accumulate points by using a plastic card every time you bet on the slots or on the table games. Ultimately, these points can be exchanged for meals at restaurants and discounts on hotel rooms (or even, in some instances, free hotel rooms), as well as for more mundane items such as mugs, T-shirts, and baseball caps. Couples who are visiting Las Vegas on a joint trip should sign up for the clubs together, in order to receive two cards that earn points credited to the same shared account.

Aiming for the Jackpot

Slot machines in the major casinos are coinless; generally you feed notes in, and will be credited with the appropriate number of plays.

When playing the slot machines, try to look for those that offer the best payback ratios (the average percentage the machine pays back to the player). Casinos like to be able to advertise themselves as having the "loosest" (highest-paying) slots, and so tend to have at least a few better-paying slots – often with signs stating "95 Percent Slots" or some such slogan – scattered amid lower-paying machines. A slot machine in a higher denomination, such as $5, will usually offer a higher return than, say, a 25-cent machine, because the casino makes a higher rate of profit from a $5 spin than it does from one of 25 cents.

In addition, choose slot machines that offer the best payout schedules – displays on the front of each machine show the payout for each winning combination, and these can vary considerably. Bear in mind that the highest jackpots tend only to be available to gamblers who play the maximum number of "lines" that each slot machine allows.

Never fall for the "It's due to hit" myth. Some gamblers imagine that a slot machine that has not paid any jackpots for a long time is due for a win. Not true. Each spin of the reels is an independent event and has nothing to do with what has gone before or will come after.

Gaming Tournaments

Keen players choose to arrange their visits to coincide with the gaming tournaments that take place year-round in Las Vegas. These tournaments are devoted to poker, video poker, slots, and blackjack. You can find full schedules on the casino websites.

The most popular are the poker tournaments. These range from the contests hosted in nearly every casino each day (almost all casinos play "No-limit Hold 'Em," with an initial buy-in for each player of between $35 and $75) via assorted three- and four-day tournaments, up to the annual World Series of Poker, which takes over the Rio Casino for seven weeks between the months of May and July. The champion of the World Series of Poker wins around $10 million.

Blackjack tournaments are also common. They generally consist of three rounds, with the winners advancing to semifinals and finals. The entry fee usually covers a certain number of tournament chips, which are issued at the start of the tournament and again before the semifinal and final rounds.

Participants in multi-day tournaments can expect to have a good deal of free time in between rounds; actual play takes up only 2 or 3 hours per day.

General Index

Acknowledgments

Author

Connie Emerson has lived in Nevada for more than 30 years, and writes travel articles for national and international publications.

Additional contributor
Greg Ward

Publishing Director Georgina Dee

Publisher Vivien Antwi

Design Director Phil Ormerod

Editorial Michelle Crane, Rebecca Flynn, Rachel Fox, Freddie Marriage, Fíodhna Ní Ghríofa, Scarlett O'Hara, Sally Schafer, Sophie Wright

Design Tessa Bindloss, Richard Czapnik

Commissioned Photography Demetrio Carrasco, Dave King, Alan Keohane, Russell MacMasters, Oliver Perez, Rough Guides/Greg Ward

Picture Research Phoebe Lowndes, Susie Peachey, Ellen Root, Lucy Sienkowska, Oran Tarjan

Cartography Suresh Kumar, Casper Morris, Reetu Pandey, John Plumer

DTP Jason Little, George Nimmo

Production Linda Dare

Factchecker Bob Barnes

Proofreader Alyse Dar

Indexer Kathryn O'Donoghue

Illustrator Chris Orr & Associates

First edition created by Blue Island Publishing, London

Revisions team Bharti Karakoti, Shikha Kulkarni, Garima Pandey, Akshay Rana, Lucy Richards, Rituraj Singh, Beverly Smart, Rachel Thompson, Vinita Venugopal

Picture Credits

4Corners: Susanne Kremer 3tl, 45b, 78-9.

akg-images: Album 37cla.

Alamy Images: AF Archive 36br; Bhandol 11br, 19tl; Pat Canova 121tr; Rob Casey 119bl; Yaacov Dagan 76tl; Ian Dagnall 11cra, 106tl; Chad Ehlers 75tr; Craig Ellenwood 69b; eye35 12cla; Lee Foster 41clb; Ted Foxx 27tr; Richard Green 20cl; Tom Arne Hanslien 103bl; D. Hurst 20-1; John Kellerman 91bl; David Kilpatrick 21tl, 24clb, 26br; Russell Kord 1; Chris Lawrence 55cb, 75bl; David Litschel 91tr; Phil Magic 18cl; Paul Maguire 11cr, 14crb; Matthew Mawson 68tl; James May 16cl; Ron Niebrugge 51tr, 65br; Planetpix 93tl; Robert Harding Picture Library/Gavin Hellier 10cla; robertharding/Michael DeFreitas 26-7, 28-9; RosalreneBetancourt 20br, 74tl; Andy Selinger 11c; Robert Shantz 29bl; Zuma Press 53b.

AWL Images: Walter Bibikow 2tr, 16-7, 34-5; Danita Delimont Stock 114-5; Michele Falzone 2tl, 8-9; Gavin Hellier 4b, 12-3; Mark Sykes 47cb; Stefano Politi Markovina 22-3.

Boulder Dam Brewing Co.: 109cla.

Caesar's Entertainment Inc.: 4t, 58br, 61cr, 63br, 67tl, 70b, 80tl, 83bl, 85tr, 85bl, 108br.

Corbis: 145/Stuart Dee 88-9; Blaine Harrington III 30br; Richard Cummins 24-5, 96cra; Lindsay Hebberd 62t; Robert Landau 25tc; Retna Ltd/Erik Kabik 60tl; Rudy Sulgan 3tr, 122-3.

The Cosmopolitan of Las Vegas: 67b.

Dorling Kindersley: Las Vegas Natural History Museum/Alan Keohane 46crb.

Dreamstime.com: Rebecca Abel 28cl; Johnny Adolphson 111tr; Alexirina27000 43t, 81br; Walter Arce 98b; Jeff Coleman 26clb; Deborah Coles 12crb; Kobby Dagan 4cla, 4cr, 11tl, 15bc, 18-9, 23bc, 25bl, 39b, 77tr; Dlabajdesign 13br, 31bl; Donyanedomam 4cl; Elvistudio 60cb; Foster Eubank 27crb; Ffooter 39tr; Anton Foltin 11crb; Larry Gevert 107cl; Helgidinson 16clb; Jabiru 30-1; Steve Lovegrove 106cb; Lunamarina 4clb; Lvphotog1 93bl; Maomaotou 36t; Maudem 14-5, Meinzahn 22cla, Juan Moyano 10cl; Derrick Neill 19br, 92cla, Nicknickko 10bl, 81tl, Nuvista 7tr; Pancaketom 110tl, 112t; Peanutroaster 6cla; Oliver Perez 84cl; Photoquest 4crb; Scott Prokop 113bl; Radkol 120b; Uros Ravbar 116cl; Gino Rigucci 28bl; Slowbird 29tl, 117tr; Snehitdesign 105t; Anthony Aneese Totah Jr 7cl; Charles Underwood 11bl; Tom Wang 74cb; Woodkern 51bl.

Eat: 95c.

Freemont Street Experience: 23tl.

Getty Images: Eugene Robert Richee 37tr; Bryan Steffy 17bc.

Golden Nugget: 94br.

Grand Canyon National Park Lodges: 118tl.

Grand Canyon Railway: 31tl.

Kemo Sabe: 21bc.

MGM Resorts International: 52cl, 65cl, 71crb,

14br, 43cr, 44clb, 58tl, 69tl; ARIA 57t, Cirque du Soleil Inc., Costumes by Dominique Lemieux 13tl.

Original Pancake House: 100br.

Palms Las Vegas: 38cra, 64b.

Robert Harding Picture Library: Kord 77cl; Eleanor Scriven 25crb; Michael Weber 16br, 22bc.

Station Casinos: 102t.

SuperStock: age fotostock 32-3; F1 Online 48-9.

Voodoo Zipline: 99cl.

Paul Wilkinson Collection: 30clb.

Wynn Las Vegas: Barbara Kraft 18br, 45tl, 55t, 64tl, 71tl, 86tl; Tomasz Rossa 57crb, 59t.

Cover
Front and spine – **Getty Images:** Mitchell Funk.

Back – **Alamy Images:** John Kellerman.

Pull Out Map Cover
Getty Images: Mitchell Funk.

All other images © Dorling Kindersley
For further information see:
www.dkimages.com

Penguin Random House

Printed and bound in China

First published in the UK in 2002
by Dorling Kindersley Limited
80 Strand, London WC2R ORL

Copyright 2002, 2018 © Dorling Kindersley Limited

A Penguin Random House Company

18 19 20 21 10 9 8 7 6 5 4 3 2 1

Reprinted with revisions 2003, 2005, 2007, 2009, 2011, 2013, 2015, 2016, 2018

ISBN 978 0 2413 1054 0

MIX
Paper from responsible sources
FSC™ C018179
www.fsc.org

SPECIAL EDITIONS OF DK TRAVEL GUIDES

DK Travel Guides can be purchased in bulk quantities at discounted prices for use in promotions or as premiums. We are also able to offer special editions and personalized jackets, corporate imprints, and excerpts from all of our books, tailored specifically to meet your own needs.

To find out more, please contact:

in the US
specialsales@dk.com

in the UK
travelguides@uk.dk.com

in Canada
specialmarkets@dk.com

in Australia
penguincorporatesales@penguinrandomhouse.com.au

As a guide to abbreviations in visitor information blocks: **Adm** = admission charge.